QUESTIONS Of The HEART

Sermons for the Middle Third of the Pentecost Season (Sundays in Ordinary Time)

Cycle B First Lesson texts from the Common Lectionary

EDWARD CHINN

C.S.S. Publishing Co., Inc.

Lima, Ohio

QUESTIONS OF THE HEART

Library of Congress Cataloging-in-Publication Data

Chinn, Edward, 1931-
Questions of the heart.

1. Episcopal Church — Sermons. 2. Anglican Communion — Sermons. 3. Sermons, American. I. Title.
BX5937.C47 1987 252'.6 87-11805
ISBN 0-89536-877-3

7863 / ISBN 0-89536-877-3

PRINTED IN U.S.A.

Table of Contents

Proper 21[1]
Pentecost 19[2]
Ordinary Time 26[3]

Is Your Religion Second-hand? 84
Job 42:1-6

[1]Common Lectionary (followed by United Methodists, Presbyterians and others)
[2]Lutheran Lectionary designation
[3]Roman Catholic Lectionary designation

All texts in this book are from the series for Lesson One, Common Lectionary. Lutheran and Roman Catholic designations indicate days comparable to Sundays on which Common Lectionary Propers are used.

Dedicated to my

Mother and Father

whose gift of life to me from God made it possible for me to ask the questions of the heart.

Introduction

Those familiar with Edward Chinn's periodic missives, *The Wonder of Words,* and his two books of the same name, will know that he is often described as a wordsmith. He takes words, examines them and puts them into theological perspective. But Edward Chinn is more than a wordsmith. He is a refiner of words who takes the raw material of language and shapes it into precise terms for better understanding.

For example, at a funeral not so long ago, Dr. Chinn spoke of the illness of the person who had died, not in the medical usage of language that called it a "terminal illness," but rather in the language of faith, calling it a "transitional illness."

In this series of sermons, the preacher speaks to the *Questions of the Heart* with definitions that clothe, enflesh, incarnate the words of faith that pose the questions we all ask and seek to understand — words such as "God," "sin," "grief," "disappointment," "wisdom," and "second-hand religion."

In this volume the reader walks and struggles along with David as shepherd boy, hero, king, sinner, disappointed parent, and dying servant of the Lord. With Job each suffers and encounters circumstances to which the standard solutions and pat answers do not fit. And with Jesus each sees anew how God takes part in the world's pain, ever offering hope and revealing insights into the questions of the heart.

Richard L. Crawford
Publisher, *The Episcopalian*

A Note Concerning Lectionaries and Calendars

The following index will aid the user of this book in matching the right Sunday with the appropriate text during the second half of the church year. Days listed here include only those appropriate to the contents of this book:

Fixed-date Lectionaries

Common	Roman Catholic	Lutheran Lectionary
Proper 12 *July 24-30*	Ordinary Time 17	Pentecost 10
Proper 13 *July 31 — August 6*	Ordinary Time 18	Pentecost 11
Proper 14 *August 7-13*	Ordinary Time 19	Pentecost 12
Proper 15 *August 14-20*	Ordinary Time 20	Pentecost 13
Proper 16 *August 21-27*	Ordinary Time 21	Pentecost 14
Proper 17 *August 28 — September 3*	Ordinary Time 22	Pentecost 15
Proper 18 *September 4-10*	Ordinary Time 23	Pentecost 16

Common	Roman Catholic	Lutheran Lectionary
Proper 19	Ordinary Time 24	Pentecost 17
September 11-17		
Proper 20	*Ordinary Time 25*	*Pentecost 18*
September 18-24		
Proper 21	Ordinary Time 26	Pentecost 19
September 25 — October 1		

Preface

A father was taking a walk with his son. The boy asked, "Daddy, what's electricity?" The father rubbed his jaw and said, "I've never known much about electricity. All I know is that it makes things run." After they had walked a little farther on, the boy said, "Daddy, how does the gasoline make the cars go?" The father kept walking and said, "Well, I don't know. You see, I don't know much about the motors in cars." The boy asked several more questions as they walked along and received the same answer. At last, the boy said, "Gee, Dad, I hope you don't mind my asking so many questions." The father smiled, put his hand on the boy's shoulder, and replied, "Not at all, son. You go right ahead and ask. How else are you going to learn anything?"

Asking questions is a sign of awareness. Henry van Dyke said that the coat of arms of his generation was the question mark. If that were true for this American clergyman who lived and wrote during the second half of the last century and the first third of this century, how much more is it true of our own generation! That is why I call this series of sermons "Questions of the Heart." These questions are prompted by the first lessons in Cycle B for the Pentecost season. Six of the lessons tell about incidents in the life of King David of Israel. The remaining four lessons are passages in the Book of Proverbs and in The Book of Job.

I want to express my appreciation to Michael L. Sherer, Editorial Director of C.S.S. Publishing Company, for his kind invitation to be part of the Lectionary Preaching Library Series; and to the Reverend Dr. Charles H. Long, Director and Editor of Forward Movement Publications, for co-publishing *The Wonder of Words* and *The Wonder of Words: Book 2*. Over the past few years, I have drawn strength from their encouragement to venture into this ministry of the written word. I am grateful also to All Saints' Episcopal Church whom I serve as pastor. Since I came to this congregation in 1960, I have spent about half my life with these dear hearts and gentle people. With them, I have sought, in preaching and by experience, to find the answers to the questions of the heart.

— Edward Chinn

Foreword

The prose of Edward Chinn was one of the pleasant discoveries for me when I came not long ago to the Diocese of Pennsylvania. Clear, uncomplicated, unpretentious, it speaks directly to the heart of human beings, laity or clergy, old or young.

Dr. Chinn has an astonishing facility in the use of illustrations. He is an inexhaustible fountain in this regard, as readers of his concise weekly essays, *"The Wonder of Words,"* know. He has already produced two collections of these thoughtful and often humorous articles in books of the same name.

This volume goes further. In these sermons Dr. Chinn draws on his rich experience as pastor of a strong congregation for more than a quarter of a century. He knows the questions which assault the souls of men and women of today. He also knows how to respond. He does so with compassion, generosity, humor, balance, and always from a soundly biblical foundation.

The reader who thought himself or herself alone with a grave question on the heart will find companionship, support, and direction in the wide range of human experience and biblical reflection which Edward Chinn spreads before him in these pages.

Allan L. Bartlett, Jr.
Bishop, Diocese of Pennsylvania

2 Samuel 12:1-14

Proper 12
Pentecost 10
Ordinary Time 17

Where Do Sins Go?

The Lord has laid on another the consequences of your sin. (2 Samuel 12:13, NEB)

On August 6, 1945, an atomic bomb was dropped on the Japanese city of Hiroshima. The light from that explosion was brighter than 25,000 suns. John Hershey wrote a book about that day. The book, titled *Hiroshima*, described the permanent shadows which were caused by the blast of that bomb. The heat from that burst of energy indelibly etched the shadows of objects and human beings upon the buildings and the roads of that place. When troops later entered that devastated city, they saw the shadow of a person who had been sitting on the steps of a bank, the shadow of a soldier unbuttoning his shirt, the shadow of a painter caught in the act of dipping his brush.

There are other shadows, too, which have an enduring quality. Shadows of personal influence remain permanently etched on human lives long after the persons themselves have gone. When Marc Antony climbed that pulpit in Rome to deliver Caesar's eulogy, he spoke eloquently of those lingering shadows of consequences: "The evil that men do lives after them." (*Julius Caesar*, III, ii, 80) If you weigh that tragic truth of evil's enduring harvest and feel its implications, then you will see how superficial are the flippant words of the nineteenth century German writer, Heinrich Heine, who said: "Of course, God will forgive me. That's his business." Heine made a fatal error by dwelling on God's forgiveness of sins, but forgetting the consequences of sins. The Psalmist reminds us: "O Lord our God, you answered them indeed; you were a God who forgave them, *yet punished them for their evil deeds*." (Psalm 99:8, *The Book of Common Prayer*)

Where do sins go? Sins go up as an iron curtain between my heart and God. "It is your sins that separate you from God," said the prophet after the days of Exile." (Isaiah 59:2, TEV) Sins also go out into the world as evil consequences. As we will see, Nathan the prophet was right when he said to King David, "The Lord has laid on another the consequences of your sin." (2 Samuel 12:13, NEB) Consider the consequences of sin in three areas: first, in David's life; secondly, in other persons' lives; thirdly, in God's life.

I

First, look at the consequences of sin in David's life. David lived about 1,000 years before Christ. He was born in Bethlehem and as a boy he distinguished himself for bravery. In one memorable moment, armed with only five stones and his shepherd's sling, he confronted and killed a taunting, giant Philistine warrior named Goliath. David was a shepherd of herds until Samuel the prophet anointed him to be the shepherd-king of Israel. He ruled as king of the tribe of Judah in Hebron for seven and a half years, then he was elected king of all the tribes. He conquered the Jebusite city of Jerusalem, made it his capital, and then won a decisive victory over the Philistine army which threatened his united Israel.

"One day, late in the afternoon, David got up from his nap and went to the palace roof. As he walked around up there, he saw a woman taking a bath in her house. She was very beautiful." (2 Samuel 11:2, TEV) In such a matter of fact way does Sacred Scripture introduce us to a turning point in David's life. The decision David made that afternoon affected the rest of his life. He sent messengers to discover who this alluring woman was. They informed him that her name was Bathsheba. She was the wife of one of David's great soldiers, a man named Uriah. David the king had Bathsheba brought to the palace where he made love to her.

The consequences of what David had done soon appeared. Bathsheba soon learned that she was pregnant. She sent a message to David telling him what had happened because of their stolen night of love. David tried desperately to hide what he had done. He sent a message to his general, Joab, who was out on the front lines of the war: "Send me Uriah the Hittite." When Uriah arrived at the palace, David asked about the progress of the war, then suggested, "Go home and rest awhile." Uriah the soldier, however, did not go home to spend the night with his wife Bathsheba. Instead, he slept at the palace gate. He avoided going home because sexual intercourse was forbidden to soldiers who were on duty. The next day David invited Uriah to supper. At the meal David succeeded in getting Uriah drunk, but the disciplined soldier still steadfastly refused to spend the night with his wife. Again, he slept at the palace.

David had failed twice in his tries to transfer to Uriah the appearance of paternity for Bathsheba's unborn child. Since Uriah was planning to return to the war zone, David wrote a letter to Joab, his general in the field. Uriah carried that letter with him as he made his way back to the fighting. He did not know that he was carrying his death sentence with him. The letter from David to Joab read: "Put Uriah in the front line, where the fighting is heaviest, then retreat and let him be killed." (2 Samuel 11:15, TEV) David's plan worked. Uriah was killed in battle. After his wife, Bathsheba, had completed the obligatory time of mourning, David took her into the palace where she became his wife and bore him a son.

Nathan the prophet came to see David. He told the king a story about a rich man who had stolen a poor man's only lamb. David became furious at this cruel act of thievery and condemned the villain of Nathan's story to death. Nathan looked at the king in silence for a moment, then pointed his finger at him and thundered, "You are that man!" The play was the thing that caught the conscience of the king. Nathan's story had dramatized for David the ugliness and injustice of his own actions with Bathsheba. "I have sinned against the Lord," said David. Nathan replied with words of solemn weight: "The Lord has laid on another the consequences of your sin." (2 Samuel 12:13, NEB) Older translations of Nathan's words read, "The Lord also has put away your sin." The New English Bible makes us aware of a dimension of forgiveness we are apt to overlook. While the forgiveness of God can restore the relationship with Him which was interrupted by sin, the terrible legacy of sin's consequences are not removed. The effects of David's sin flowed into Bathsheba's life, into the life of her little child, into the life of her husband, Uriah, and on into David's family, where his sons no longer felt the weight of his moral authority. Where do sins go? They spread out through the fabric of human relationships like a dark, offensive stain.

II

Secondly, look at the consequences of sin in other persons' lives. Almeda Adams was the blind author of a book titled *Seeing Europe Through Sightless Eyes*. She helped to establish the Cleveland Music School Settlement. How did she become blind? When she was one day old, she was treated in the hospital by a doctor who had committed the sin of gluttony by overindulging in alcohol. In drunken stupor, the doctor had gone to the hospital where he was scheduled to be on duty. Because his judgment was impaired by his excessive drinking, he put too strong a solution of silver nitrate in little Almeda Adams' eyes. Because of his sin, this woman has spent her entire life in perpetual darkness. If that doctor had invoked Heinrich Heine's words ("Of course, God will forgive me;

that's his business''), he, too, would have been blind, blind to the serious consequences of his sin. Nathan the prophet was right about the inevitably interrelated nature of this world when he said to David, ''The Lord has laid on another the consequences of your sin.''

The consequences of one person's sin in the life of another person is seen with particular pathos indeed in a new-born baby who suffers from drug addiction. A writer in genetics, Amran Scheinfeld, has described what happens: ''Various drugs may pass from the mother to the embryo. If she smokes or drinks to excess, the nicotine or alcohol in her system may reach the child with harmful, even disastrous effects . . . Especially dangerous are narcotics. If the mother is addicted to the point where her tissues are saturated with the drug, the child may come into the world as a drug addict.''

A man with a troubled conscience went to his pastor for advice. The man had gossiped about an acquaintance, then learned that his words were not only unkind, but also untrue. The man asked the pastor what he could do to make amends. The pastor told him, ''If you want to profit spiritually, you must fill a bag with goose feathers, then go to every door in the neighborhood and drop a feather on each porch.'' The man got a bag, filled it with feathers, and did as he had been told. Then he went back to the pastor and asked, ''Is that all I need to do?'' The pastor replied, ''No, that is not all! Now take the bag and go back and gather up every feather you dropped.'' The man went away. After a long time, he came back and said, ''Pastor, I can't find all the feathers I dropped because the wind has blown them far and wide.'' The pastor replied, ''That is how it is with the sin of gossip.'' Unkind words are so easily dropped, but we can never take them back! The consequences of our words flow outward beyond your reach into other people's lives. The Lord has laid on another the consequences of your sin.

III

Thirdly, look at the consequences of sin in God's life. In the sixth century before Christ, two men, hundreds of miles apart, had the same intuition that sin's consequences touched God. In Greece, Aeschylus wrote about Prometheus, the son of one of the Titans of Greek mythology. Jupiter, the father of gods, gave Prometheus the task of creating man. Prometheus went to the bank of a river in Arcadia, scooped up clay, molded it into the figure of a man, and breathed into it the breath of life. Prometheus then wondered what gift he might give this new creature. Prometheus' brother had created the animals and given them the gifts of cunning, speed, strength, claws, and shells. Finally, Prometheus decided to give to man the divine gift of fire wherewith man would be able to make tools, fashion weapons, and warm his home. Jupiter, the father of gods, however, would not allow fire to be given to man. Prometheus, therefore, stole the fire from heaven and gave it to man. In punishment for his sin, Jupiter chained Prometheus to a rock on Mount Caccasus. Every day an eagle came and ate Prometheus' liver; every night his liver regrew. Prometheus lived in perpetual pain. Now listen to the words of Hermes, the messenger of the gods, who came to Prometheus and said to him: "Look not for any end, moreover, to this curse until some god appears to accept upon his head the pangs of thy own sins vicarious." Six hundred years before Christ, Aeschylus, the Greek dramatist, saw that the consequences of sin were so great that in some way they would touch even divinity.

In Judah, Isaiah of Babylon, had the same insight about the Suffering Servant of God:

Yet on himself he bore our
sufferings,
our torments he endured,
while we counted him smitten by
God,

struck down by disease and
misery;
but he was pierced for our
transgressions,
tortured for our iniquities;
the chastisement he bore is health
for us
and by his scourging we are healed.
We had all strayed like sheep,
each of us had gone his own way;
but the Lord laid upon him
the guilt of us all . . .
After all his pains he shall be
bathed in light,
after his disgrace he shall be fully
vindicated;
so shall he, my servant, vindicate
many,
himself bearing the penalty of their
guilt.
Therefore I will allot him a portion
with the great,
and he shall share the spoil with
the mighty,
because he exposed himself to face
death
and was reckoned among
transgressors,
because he bore the sin of many
and interceded for their
transgressions."

Isaiah 53:4-6, 11-12, NEB.

The consequences of sin do not only affect you; they do not only run out and affect other persons. In the Cross of Christ, we see that even God is touched by the consequences of our sins. The God of Mount Calvary is different from the gods of Mount Olympus! The God and Father of our Lord Jesus Christ is not an indifferent Spectator untouched by the world's pain; He is an active Participant in the world's suffering, bearing on his own heart the consequences of our sins. "The Cross is a translation into history of an eternal fact," wrote the late Leslie Weatherhead. In one of his books, Dr. Weatherhead recalled a night when his ship sailed past the island of Stromboli, off the coast of Sicily. He saw the bright fires of the Strombolian volcano light up the black sky. "Just as the flash of the volcano reveals the fires forever burning in the mountain's heart," wrote Dr. Weatherhead, "so the incident [of the cross of Christ] on Calvary two thousand years ago shows the nature of the eternal God."

I sometimes think about the Cross,
And shut my eyes and try to see
The cruel nails and crown of thorns,
And Jesus crucified for me.

But even could I see Him die,
I could but see a little part
Of that great love which like a fire
Is always burning in His heart.

Heinrich Heine said, "Of course, God will forgive me; that's his business!" But, dealing with human sin is not that simple, is it? Look at the Cross and see that the consequences of sin run up to touch even God, who is involved up to his scarprints!

2 Samuel 12:15b-24

Proper 13
Pentecost 11
Ordinary Time 18

When Things Don't Work Out, What Then?

A week later the child died, and David's officials were afraid to tell him the news." (2 Samuel 12:18, TEV)

When things don't work out, what then? An old man looked back over his life and said, "I have had a great many disappointments, but the greatest of them is the disappointment I had as a boy. When I was a boy, I crawled under a tent to see a circus and discovered that I was in a revival meeting!" There are many instances in our life of this matter of disappointment. A bride and groom walk out of a church after a beautiful wedding ceremony with great dreams and high hopes of their future life together, but things don't always work out. Death or divorce may intervene. Young parents bring their first child to be baptized. They have marvelous plans for this new life, but forty years later the mother says, "I'm so disappointed in my son. Things didn't work out with him as we had hoped." I heard a man who was approaching retirement, as he surveyed his life, say, "If I had it to do all over again, I would never have gone into the line of work that I did." Things did not work out for him.

The Bible holds up a mirror to our human condition and reflects this common experience of disappointment when things don't work out. Moses, for example, spent most of his life leading his people from Egypt to the land of Promise. He looked forward to entering that land with his people, but things didn't work out that way. He was not permitted to enter that land. Again, old King David, a thousand years before Christ, dreamed of building a great Temple in Jerusalem to be the sanctuary of the Holy One of Israel. That was David's great dream, but things did not work out that way. It fell to his son Solomon to build that magnificent Temple. Again, the apostle Paul wrote these words to the Christians in Rome: "I would like to see you on my way to Spain." (Romans 15:24, TEV) Paul had cherished plans to go to Spain, but he never reached there. He ended up, instead, in a jail cell in Rome.

When we face this question of what to do when things don't work out, we are dealing with a problem that human beings have had to face over the centuries. Look at how King David faced that matter when his little son became sick. Bathsheba, the wife of David's general, Uriah, had borne a child to David. David had repented of his adultery with Uriah's wife, but that repentance and the subsequent absolution pronounced by the prophet Nathan did not remove the consequences of David's act. Nathan pointed out that what David had done was unworthy of a prince of Israel who was greatly indebted to God. God's punishment for David's sin was to be twofold. First, there was the sword. Uriah had died by the sword. From that time on, David and his family would suffer from the sword. Secondly, David would lose the child who was the fruit of his sin with Bathsheba. "The Lord caused the child that Uriah's wife had borne to David to become very sick." (2 Samuel 12:15, TEV)

It is difficult for us who know God through Jesus Christ to accept this bare statement that the child's illness and death were the result of God's direct action. Later in the history of Israel, the Book of Job would wrestle with the neat equation that misfortune invariably means God's Punishment. Later the prophet Micah would question whether God really wants a man's child as the price of his forgiveness: "Shall I offer him my first-born child to pay for my sins?." (Micah 6:7, TEV) Contrast the view of the author of 2 Samuel, who interpreted the child's illness as God's curse, with the clear statement of our Lord Jesus who said: "It is not the will of my Father who is in heaven that one of these little ones should perish." (Matthew 18:14, RSV) However hard it is for us to reconcile this story of a child struck down with illness by God with the picture of the God we see in Christ, this narrative about David's child brings home to us two insights most clearly: for one thing, deeply imbedded in Old Testament thought is the idea of the God whose sense of justice causes him to repay every man for his deeds; for another thing, sin takes on a life of its own as its effects spread out to engulf the innocent and the guilty alike. Not even David's repentance can remove the bitter fact of consequences.

David shared this problem of disappointment. "David prayed to God that the child would get well." (2 Samuel 12:16) He refused to eat and spent the nights lying on the floor of his room. His court officials tried to comfort him and get him to eat and rest properly, but he refused their efforts. "A week later the child died, and David's officials were afraid to tell him the news." (2 Samuel 12:18) When David learned of the child's death, he refused to observe the customary rites of mourning. Instead, he washed, changed his clothes, went to worship at the house of the Lord and then came home and ate a hearty meal. David, too, knew what it meant to face a situation where things don't work out as he had hoped that they would. In his disappointment, David did three things. First, he checked for a message. Secondly, he changed his outlook. Thirdly, he chose to keep on trusting God.

I

What can we do when things don't work out? First, we can check for a message. When David's hopes for the child's survival did not work out, David "entered the house of the Lord and prostrated himself there." (2 Samuel 12:20, NEB) In the Book of the Psalms ascribed to David, there is an account of a person who, like David, tried to understand the hard facts of life:

I tried to think this problem
through.
but it was too difficult for me
until I went into your Temple.
Then I understood . . . (Psalm 73:16-17, TEV)

David put himself into the environment where he was open to hear God speak his message. When things don't work out, we can ask the question: What is God saying to me in this situation? When the apostle Paul was on his second missionary journey, he planned to go to the province of Bithynia in Asia Minor along the bottom of the Black Sea, not far from his home town of Tarsus. Paul wanted to take the Christian message to Asia Minor. That was his plan. However, when we look at the travel diary of Luke, the diary which grew into Luke's second volume, *The Acts of the Apostles*, we see that Paul, too, had to face this fact that things don't always work out as we had planned. Luke wrote this: "When they reached the border of Mysia, they tried to go into the province of Bithynia, but the Spirit of Jesus did not allow them." In some way, circumstances made it clear that this was not what Christ wanted. Imagine Paul's disappointment. He wanted to take the Good News of Christ into Asia Minor. Instead, he had to make a left-hand turn and go to Troas, a seaport city on the eastern edge of the Aegean Sea. That night in Troas, when he went to sleep, Paul found a message in his disappointment. He dreamed about a man who stood in Macedonia, the near edge of Europe, across that Aegean Sea. The man called out to him, "Come over to Macedonia and help us!" (Acts 16:9, TEV) In his disappointment Paul discovered that God had a new appointment in mind for him. God gave to Paul a new experience that he would not have had if Paul had had his way and went to Asia Minor. God said to Paul, "I have a better idea. In your disappointment, look again. Here is a new appointment for you. I will open Europe to your message." That is how the Gospel traveled westward to Rome, to Spain, to Britain, and, eventually, to us. When things don't work out, check for a message. Even in our disappointment, there is an answer to our prayers. The answer may be that, in this disappointment, God is making a new appointment with us for a whole new experience which will be greater and better than our original plan.

II

Secondly, when things don't work out, we can change our outlook. When David's hopes for his child did not happen, he changed his outlook. That change is reflected in his behavior.

> *When he returned to the palace, he asked for food and ate it as soon as it was served. "We don't understand this," his officials said to him. "While the child was alive, you wept for him and would not eat; but as soon as he died, you got up and ate!"*
>
> *"Yes," David answered, "I did fast and weep while he was still alive. I thought that the Lord might be merciful to me and not let the child die. But now that he is dead, why should I fast? Could I bring the child back to life? I will some day go to where he is, but he can never come back to me." (2 Samuel 12:20-23, TEV)*

In 1915 in Coffee County, Alabama, the people were disappointed because the cotton harvest was an utter failure. The failure was caused by a little beetle that got inside the seed pods and ate the plant. The beetle was called the boll weevil. That year the cotton crop was destroyed. What should they do? Then, a black man named George Washington Carver picked up a peanut and said, "God, show me all the possibilities that are in this peanut." After experimentation, Carver discovered a host of new uses for the peanut. He then went to Coffee County, Alabama, and persuaded the citizens there to change their outlook and their approach. Instead of planting cotton, they began to plant peanuts. Four years later those people were on their way to prosperity. Enthusiastic about their new outlook and approach, they erected the only known monument to a beetle in the world. The monument reads: "In profound appreciation of the boll weevil and what it has done as the herald of prosperity, this monument is erected by the citizens of Enterprise, Coffee County, Alabama." In their disappointment over a ruined harvest of cotton, they found something even better. When things don't work out, what then? Change your outlook and your approach.

Isn't that what we have to do in the area of physical health? If things are not working out for you in matters of health, the doctor will tell you, "You've got to change your diet. You've got to change your outlook. You've got to change your whole style of living. Unless you do this, you will die." Now, in that circumstance, we can't blame God if we continue to be sick. We have not changed what we should change to see God's good purpose of health realized in our lives. When things don't work out, what then? Then you have to change your attitude, your outlook, and your approach to living.

III

Thirdly, when things don't work out, we can choose to keep on trusting God. David did not take his grief out on Bathsheba, nor did he stop believing that God had a plan for his life. Instead, David consoled Bathsheba and not long afterwards, she gave birth to a son who was given the significant name "Jedidiah" Beloved of the Lord!

In the Book of Daniel in the Old Testament, we are told that King Nebuchadnezzar of Babylon ordered that everyone should bow down to a gold statue he had set up in the plain of Dura. However, three Hebrew young men refused to obey the king. They were Shadrach, Meshach, and Abednego. They said to the king, "Your Majesty, we will not try to defend ourselves. If the God whom we serve is able to save us from the blazing furnace and from your power, then he will. But even if he doesn't, Your Majesty may be sure that we will not worship your god . . ." (Daniel 3:16-18, TEV) When God doesn't deliver you or your loved one from the problem, even then you can choose to hold on and to keep on trusting God.

Leslie Weatherhead has given us a striking image of this type of trust in God. He has reminded us that a skeptic could formulate a list of charges against God which would call his character into serious question. The earthly parallel to this, says Weatherhead, is the list of charges which a person could formulate against a great surgeon and present to the surgeon's five year old son. "Do you know," one could say to the son, "that your father gets a person unconscious on a table, and when he is unconscious and can't defend himself, your father cuts open his body with a sharp knife and cuts out part of it and throws it away? What do you think of a father who would do such a thing? What would you think if your father did this to you?" On the surface, the son might admit that such a list of things like this wouldn't work out to be the expected portrait of a loving father. But, the son could choose to say, "I can't understand all that, but I know my father. I know that he is kind and good and would never do anything to hurt anybody. Though the things you say against my surgeon-father may be true, I still choose to keep on trusting him!" Likewise, when things don't work out, we can choose to keep on trusting God.

This kind of trust was the secret of Christ's inner power. Sometimes, we forget that things didn't always work out for him, either. He had to face failures. The cause of the failures was not in himself; it was in the persons and circumstances with which he was dealing. For example, he went back to his hometown of Nazareth, but things didn't work out as he had hoped. He failed to get a positive response from most of the people who knew him there when he was growing to manhood. "He was not able to perform any miracles there, except that he placed his hands on a few sick people and healed them. He was greatly surprised, because the people there did not have faith." (Mark 6:5-6, TEV) Furthermore, he failed to win his nation Israel to his way. During the last week of his life, he spoke of his nation's capital: "Jerusalem, Jerusalem . . . How many times I wanted to put my arms around all your people, just as a hen gathers her chicks under her wings, but you would not let me." (Matthew 21:37, TEV) When he was being watched by hostile critics; when he was being cross-examined by his enemies; when he was in distress of soul as he faced the possibility of having to drink the cup of suffering; when he faced the unanswered question, "My God, my God, why hast thou forsaken me?" (Mark 15:34, NEB), Christ chose to keep on trusting in One who was his Father. "Father, into thy hands I commit my spirit." (Luke 23:46, NEB)

Things don't always work out in the way we had hoped and planned that they would. An American educator, Jean Fleming Brown, summed up this experience this way: "No man, with a man's heart in him, gets far on his way without some bitter, soul-searching disappointment. Happy is he who is brave enough to push on another stage of the journey. . ." When this is your experience, as it was old King David's, you can do three things: check for a message; change your outlook and approach; and choose to keep on trusting God.

2 Samuel 18:1, 5, 9-15

Proper 14
Pentecost 12
Ordinary Time 19

What Is God Like?

"Deal gently with the young man Absalom for my sake." (2 Samuel 18:5, NEB)

When Harry Truman was President of the United States, his daughter Margaret gave a concert in Washington, D.C. The next day Paul Hume, music critic of the *Washington Post*, gave her performance a bad review. Characteristically, Harry Truman did not let that slight of his daughter's singing pass without comment. He wrote a letter to Paul Hume. In that letter, Truman wrote: "I have read your lousy review of Margaret's concert. I've come to the conclusion that you are an 'eight ulcer man on four ulcer pay.' Someday I hope to meet you. When that happens you'll need a new nose, and a lot of beefsteak for black eyes . . ." Truman was the kind of father who stood up for his children.

Is God like that? Harry Emerson Fosdick, in his book *Dear Mr. Brown*, wrote these words: "We cannot possibly jump outside of our human experience and find any terms with which to describe God except such terms as our day-to-day living provides. All our thinking about God has to be done with pictures, symbols, images, drawn from human experience." One day Frederick Myers, the English philosopher, was asked, "If you could put one question to the great Sphinx in Egypt and be assured of an answer, what would that question be?"

After a moment's thought, Myers replied with this question for the Sphinx: "Is this universe friendly?" That is the question, isn't it? People have argued whether God exists. If, when you use the word *God*, you mean power, creative power, then there is no argument about the existence of that. Everywhere you can see the evidence of creative power sweeping through our universe and out beyond the margins of the stars and the frontiers of thought. The haunting questions that confront us when we look into the face of a newborn baby or into the blackness of an open grave is this: Does that power care about us? What is that power like?

In answer to that question, Christian faith accepts Christ's word: "You have a Father . . ." (Luke 12:30, NEB) We can explore the implications of God as father by looking at three persons in the Bible: David's son, Absalom; David himself; and David's greater Son, Christ.

I

First, look at David's son, Absalom, and see what God as father has to deal with. Absalom was David's third son. He had a sister named Tamar. She was a beautiful young woman. Tamar's half-brother, Amnon, fell in love with her. His desire for her was so great that he became ill. His cousin, Jonadab, told him to pretend he was sick and to ask his father David to let Tamar bring him food. Amnon followed his cousin's advice, asked David for that favor, and it was granted. When Tamar came to his room, he raped her. Absalom was infuriated at what Amnon had done to his sister, but he waited to take his revenge. Two years later Absalom gave a party to celebrate the time of sheep shearing. He told his servants to wait until Amnon was drunk, then to kill him. When old King David heard that his son Amnon had been murdered at the direction of his other son, Absalom, he was broken-hearted. Absalom ran away and lived for three years in self-imposed exile. Then, David's friend and general, Joab, interceded for him with the King. David gave permission for Absalom to return to Jerusalem, but refused to see him. Two years passed, then David relented and welcomed Absalom back.

Absalom used his favorable standing with the King to begin a new strategy. He stood at the city gate. As people came to plead their cases before the King, Absalom met them and said, "I can see that you are right in this matter; it's unfortunate that the King doesn't have anyone to assist him in hearing these cases. I surely wish I were judge; then anyone with a lawsuit could come to me and I would give him justice." (2 Samuel 15:3-4, The Living Bible) By this approach to the people, Absalom undermined his father's position. In a memorable phrase, the Scripture says: "So in this way Absalom stole the hearts of all the people of Israel." (2 Samuel 15:6, The Living Bible)

Gradually, Absalom built up a following in the nation. Then, he declared open rebellion against the king, his father David. He organized the army of Israel and led an attack against David who was forced to escape from his capital. Among the trees of the forest of Ephraim, the two contestants found their final battlefield. Isn't that what God as father has to deal with? He, too, has had to face his rebellious offspring. In the imagery of the Book of Genesis, there is Adam in the garden, standing by the tree of the knowledge of good and evil and shaking his fist at the heavens. Adam rebelled. Sin is rebellion. It is obstinate resistance. It is a refusal to do what God has commanded. Again, in the imagery of the Gospel, there is the Second Adam on the tree of the cross as the descendants of the first Adam are gathered around that tree to challenge God's authority.

When we think of Absalom's rebellion, we understand the personal nature of sin more clearly. We see what God has to deal with. When sin is described as "transgression," it remains impersonal. It is the stepping over the line drawn by the law. But, to think of sin as "rebellion" involves thinking of sin as a revolt against a person. In his autobiography

Treasure in Clay, the late Roman Catholic Bishop Fulton J. Sheen wrote: "No one who exceeds the speed limit ever leans over the steering wheel when he drives into the garage and says an Act of Contrition. But, when we compromise, in any way, the love of Christ in the soul . . . we then know sin as *hurting someone we love.*"

II

Secondly, look at David himself and see how God as father cares. In the forest of Ephraim, David stood ready to confront his son Absalom and the Israeli army whom Absalom had won to his side. Listen as David speaks to his generals: "Deal gently with the young man Absalom for my sake." (2 Samuel 18:5, NEB) Critics of David say that David was wrong in his concern for his son. Some Bible commentaries say that David was putting the interests of his traitorous, rebellious son ahead of his duty to the nation. They say that because he was the king he should have not been so kind to Absalom. Other critics of David say that he could not have disciplined Absalom as he should, because David himself had lost his moral authority when he sinned with Bathsheba. When we have granted these critics the validity of their statements about David, can't we still sympathize with a father's heart here? Despite the fact that his son had committed murder and led a rebellion against him, this father persisted in caring for his son: "Deal gently with the young man Absalom for my sake."

Among the Psalms which are related to David and to incidents in his life is Psalm 103. That psalm praises God for his mercy and unchanging love. Maybe David had learned the lesson of God's fatherly care in the absolution he had heard pronounced by Nathan, that word of forgiveness to David for his sin with Bathsheba. Anyhow, the author of that psalm surely expressed David's feeling when he wrote:

As far as the east is from the west,
so far does he remove our sins from us.
As a father is kind to his children,
so the Lord is kind to those who honor him.
He knows what we are made of;
he remembers that we are dust." (Psalm 103:12-14, TEV)

III

Thirdly, look at David's greater Son, Christ, and see what God as father is like. In first century Rome, an Emperor celebrated a victorious military campaign by leading his troops through the streets of the capital. Along the route, a platform had been erected where the Empress and the Emperor's family could sit and observe the procession. As that procession approached the platform, the Emperor's little son jumped down from the Platform, squeezed through the crowd, and started to run out on the road to meet his father's chariot. A Roman soldier who was guarding the road spotted the boy, did not recognize him, held him back, saying, "You can't run out there! Don't you know that's the emperor?" The boy laughed and replied, "He may be your emperor, but he's my father!"

In this old story, retold in a book by William Barclay, is an excellent example of Jesus' attitude to God as father. When Jesus prayed to God, he called Him by the Aramaic word *Abba* (Mark 14:36). This word abba has a warmer shade of meaning than merely father. It is the word that a little child in first century Palestine would use when he was addressing his earthly father in the intimacy of the family. "There is," wrote Dr. Barclay, "only one possible English translation of this word in any ordinary use, and that is 'Daddy.' " No Jew in Jesus' day would have dared to use that word *Abba* for God. Ponder, then what this word says about David's greater Son, Jesus, when you realize that Jesus called God *Abba* and taught his followers to do the same (Romans 8:15; Galatians 4:6).

Christ told a story about a rebellious son who was like Absalom. In that Parable of the Prodigal Son, he sketched a portrait of another son who misused his freedom, rebelled against his father's ways, left home, and spent his substance in riotous living in the far country. When that son came to his senses, he started back home. "He was still a long way from home," said Jesus, "when his father saw him; his heart was filled with pity and he ran, threw his arms around his son, and kissed him." (Luke 15:20, TEV) When the older son, who was working in the field, looked up, he was dumbfounded. His father had thrown all sense of dignity to the winds. Look at that father *running* — his robe flapping in the breeze, his beard bouncing on his chest, his sandals smacking the road. Christ's meaning is crystal clear. If David could ask his generals to deal gently with erring Absalom, how much more does the love of the heavenly Father know no bounds. In effect Jesus was saying: "What I do represents God's nature and purpose. I am acting as God's representative." If it seems undignified to see Christ associating with prostitutes and racketeers, that's how God's undignified love always looks. It looks as undignified as a king like David, who had to flee as a fugitive, but was forgiving as a father. It looks as undignified as a father running wildly down the road to welcome his returning son. That divine love comes running down among us into the most undignified places! That love came running down to a shepherd boy named David and made him the shepherd of Israel, forgiving him his failures and using him for divine purposes. Centuries later, in the fullness of time and at the crossroads of the world, God's love came running down into a foul stable at Bethlehem and ended up naked and writhing on a cross at Calvary to show us what *Abba* is really like.

A few years ago there was a letter in Ann Lander's syndicated newspaper column from a woman who signed herself, "78 And Still Praying." She wrote:

For years, I have been horrified by a children's prayer that has become part of our culture.

"Now I lay me down to sleep,

I pray the Lord my soul to keep.
If I should die before I wake
I pray the Lord my soul to take."

I doubt that a small child relates "Lord" to God, nor would he have any concept of what "soul" means. What's more, suggesting to a child that he might die in his sleep seem unnecessarily cruel. I have written an alternative prayer that I feel has more merit. I can think of no better way to spread the words than through your column. I hope you will deem it worthy.

"We've come to the end of another day,
Hear me, dear Father, as I pray.
Thank thee for all the blessings we share
And keep me in thy loving care."

That modern prayer comes close to the way a little Jewish child in Jesus' day addressed God at bedtime. Before that child closed his eyes in sleep, he would say these words from Psalm 31:6 — "Into thy hands I commend my spirit." When David's greater Son, Christ, was ready to close his eyes in the sleep of death as he hung on the cross, his mind went back to that childhood prayer. Again, he quoted those words, but with one significant addition. He prefaced those words with his favorite name for God, the name *Abba*, dear Father: "Father, into your hands I commend my spirit."

When we look at David and hear his plea, "Deal gently with the young man Absalom for my sake," we have a glimpse through a father's heart at the great heart of God as father. When we see David dealing with his fatherly love and his son's misused freedom, we recognize how deeply the cross is imbedded in the grain of personal life as a heartfelt experience, as well as an historical fact. As believers in a heavenly Father, who has not been perplexed and pained at evil? There are the natural evils of cyclones, cancer, birth defects, earthquakes. There are the moral evils of pride, anger, lust, indifference, envy, greed, and gluttony. An old Greek philosopher, Epicurus, stated the problem well when he asked, "Is Deity willing to prevent evil, but not able? Then he is impotent. Is he able to prevent evil, but not willing? Then he is malevolent. Is he both able and willing? Whence then is evil?'' In this episode in David's life and in the cross of David's greater Son, Christ, we see the awful mysteries of human freedom and the love of God as father.

> *What is love? Love is the power to grant freedom without desiring to limit or inhibit its exercise. It is the power to give freedom without any will to take it back. And it is only Omnipotence that can refrain absolutely from trespassing upon freedom. Only God can give and not take back. . . He suffers within Himself the entire consequence of allowing man absolute freedom. That is His Love . . .*
>
> *Thus the existence of evil and suffering in the world is a proof, not that God is either Good but powerless, or All Powerful but not good. On the contrary, it is a proof that God is both loving and omnipotent. Only absolute love could grant unhindered freedom, and only omnipotence could endure the operation of that freedom.*
>
> *— D. R. Davies*

2 Samuel 18:24-33

Proper 15
Pentecost 13
Ordinary Time 20

How Can We Meet Grief?

The king was overcome with grief. He went up to his room over the gateway and wept. As he went he cried, "O my son, my son, Absalom, Absalom, my son, if only I had died in your place, my son." (2 Samuel 18:33 TEV)

Across thirty centuries, comes this cry of grief from David, whom God called from being a shepherd of herds to be the shepherd of His people, Israel. David had a son named Absalom. Absalom had murdered his brother because that brother had raped his sister, Tamar. After being accepted back into the family, Absalom had led a rebellion against his father, the king. That rebel son had won the Israeli army to his side. In a dramatic showdown in the woods of Ephraim, Absalom rode through the forest away from his father's men, when suddenly his mule went beneath the thick boughs of a great oak tree, and his hair was caught in the branches. His mule went on, leaving Absalom dangling in the air. David's men told General Joab what had happened to Absalom. They were reluctant to kill the young man because David had instructed them to deal gently with him. " 'Enough of this nonsense,' Joab said. Then he took three daggers and plunged them into the heart of Absalom as he dangled alive from the oak. Ten of Joab's young armor beárers then surrounded Absalom and finished him off." (2 Samuel 18:14-15, The Living Bible) A messenger brought the news of Absalom's death to King David. "The king was overcome with grief. He went up to his room over the gateway and wept. As he went he cried, 'O my son, my son, Absalom, Absalom, my son, if only I had died in your place, my son." (2 Samuel 18:33, TEV) When a child buries his parent, he is burying the past. But, when a parent buries his child, he is burying the future. As we look at David sobbing out his grief, consider two questions: What is grief? How can we meet grief?

"I am worn out with grief," wrote the Psalmist. "Every night my bed is damp from my weeping; my pillow is soaked with tears. I can hardly see; my eyes are swollen from my weeping." (Psalm 6:6, TEV) What is grief? The word *grief* comes from the Latin word "gravis," meaning "heavy." When you grieve, you have a heavy heart. The heaviness comes from four feelings. First, you feel deprived because you have lost someone dear to you. Secondly, you feel disbelieving. Under the shock of the loss, you feel numb and you deny the reality of what has happened. "It can't be," you're apt to say. Thirdly, you feel depressed. The depression appears as an attitude of hopelessness, emptiness, and a lack of interest in what's going on around you. Fourthly, you feel devitalized by negative emotions. About the past, you may feel guilt about things done or left undone. About the present, you may feel anger at the attending doctors, the hospital, other family members, or even God. About the future, you may feel worry about how you will be able to carry on without the person who has died.

I

How can we meet grief? There are four things that we can do as we confront the emotion of grief. Each of these four actions begins with the letter "D." First, consider the word "Declare." You can meet grief by declaring it. Why do people try to hide their grief? Sometimes, no doubt, it is because they are unwilling to add the weight of their grief to the woes already being carried by other people. Furthermore, people who do not declare their grief may fear that the sympathy they will receive from others who see them vent their grief will dissolve their own self-control. Still another reason people do not declare their grief is because of pride. They enjoy the reputation of strength which unexpressed grief earns them. As an unknown poet has written:

They call me strong because my tears I shed where none can see,
Because I smile, tell merry tales, and win the crowds to me.
They call me strong because I laugh to ease an aching heart,
Because I keep the sweet side out, and hide the bitter part.

In William Shakespeare's play, *Macbeth*, a character named MacDuff had just learned that his wife and children have been murdered. His friend Malcolm advises MacDuff to declare his grief: "Give sorrow words. The grief that does not speak whispers the o'er-fraught heart and bids it break." (IV, 3, 209) Remember that memorable scene in John's account of the Gospel. As Christ stood at the tomb of Lazarus, his friend, he declared his grief by crying. Such an outward expression of grief by Christ contradicts the advice of some misguided parents who tell their sons, "Big boys don't cry." A psychologist has stated that some boys at age ten have been so conditioned by their parents that they do not dare to cry. When one of those boys reaches the age of twenty, he doesn't even think of crying when he has experienced disappointment because his girl friend has jilted him or he has been dropped from college. When this young man has reached the age of forty, says the psychologist, he doesn't even know *how* to cry. However, though unexpressed by words, that grief may leak out as physical illness.

II

Secondly, consider the word "Delight." You can meet grief by delighting in the memory of those good experiences you shared with the departed person. In the Middle Ages, many persons sought a magical chemical which would have the power to transform some base metal, such as lead, into gold. This combination of chemistry, magic, and philosophy was called alchemy. In a figurative sense, there is a magic-like element that can transform ordinary grief into "good grief." That element is gratitude. Go back over your life in memory and think of what you shared with that person whom you loved and have lost awhile. Then, give thanks to God for all the good experiences which flowed into your life because of that departed person. You will find that such gratitude can put a healing balm on your grieving soul.

In a certain town, there was a woman who was a busybody. One day she met the town lawyer on Main Street. She tried to get information out of him about the death of the town's richest man. "You knew him well," she cooed. "How much wealth did he leave?" The old lawyer tipped his hat and replied, "All of it, madam, all of it!" Not only do our loved ones leave their wealth behind; they leave behind them, too, the memory of their words and their example. In quiet moments, we reflect with gratitude on what their lives have meant on us to our own journey.

During the Civil War, there was a stockade at Andersonville, in southwestern Georgia. The log stockade enclosed only sixteen acres, but as many as 30,000 Northern prisoners at a time were crowded into that small space! More than 12,000 graves witness to the dreadful conditions there. In Wisconsin, there is a monument in memory of the 378 young men from that state who died in the Andersonville stockade. On the monument are lines written by Thomas Campbell. As we delight in the happy memory of our loved ones, we can make those words our own:

And is he dead, whose glorious mind
Lifts thine on high?
To live in hearts we leave behind
Is not to die.

III

Thirdly, consider the word "Dedicate." You can meet grief by dedicating yourself to doing something for other persons who are hurting. "When I dig another person out of trouble," says an old Chinese proverb, "the hole from which I lift him is the place where I bury my own trouble." Leslie Weatherhead, the late English preacher, grieved for his mother after she died. One day he picked up her Bible and found strengthening words written on the flyleaf of that Bible. Here are those words:

If I should die, and leave you here awhile,
Be not like others sore undone, who keep
Long vigils by the silent dust and weep.
For my sake, turn again to life, and smile,
Nerving thy heart and trembling hand to do
Something to comfort weaker hearts than thine.
Complete these dear unfinished tasks of mine,
And I, perchance, may therein comfort you!

In his book *How To Be A Transformed Person*, E. Stanley Jones wrote: "Meister Eckhart said, 'God's every affliction is a lure' — a lure to help you to help others. You are made tender by your sorrow, and that tenderness can make your service tenderly effective." Dr. Jones illustrated that quotation by telling the story of Josephine Butler. This woman had only one child whom she loved very much. One day, as Josephine Butler arrived home in her carriage, this little girl ran to the railing and fell, dying at her mother's feet. In her grief, she went to an old Quaker man who taught her to transform her dejection into dedication. The Quaker said: "God has taken to himself her whom thou didst love: but there are many forlorn young hearts who need that mother love of thine." At the instruction of the Quaker gentleman, she went to a house which had been turned into a refuge. Forty young people were being cared for in that place. Dr. Jones commented: "Josephine Butler threw herself into that service and became one of the greatest social reformers of the century. She didn't bear her grief; she set it to music."

IV

Fourthly, consider the word "Decide." You can meet grief by deciding to look at life and death from the perspective of Jesus Christ. The late German theologian Helmut Thielicke wrote these words in his book *How To Believe*: "For basically faith is nothing else than a certain way of looking at things." Just as the negative faith of atheism is essentially a certain way of looking at life, so the faith of the Christian is looking at life through the eyes of Christ who said, "Let not your heart be troubled; you believe in God, believe also in Me. In My Father's house are many mansions; if it were not so, I would have told you." (John 14:1-2, NKJV) The imagery which Christ used in these words comes from the travel arrangements in the first century. Along the roads, there were "mansions" at regular stages of a traveler's journey. These places were not "mansions" in our sense of the word, but simply accomodations for travelers. A traveler would make his way along that road until the shadows lengthened and the evening came. Then, he would stop at one of those mansions to rest for the night. The next morning he would resume his journey and travel another stage of his journey. In effect, Christ was saying to us, "Within my Father's world, there are many "stations" marking the stages of growth in the journey of a soul. If it were not so, I surely would have told you." Because of Christ, God's children never see one another for the *last* time!

This way of looking at life accounts for the note of joy and triumph among the early Christians whom St. Augustine called "the Easter People." In A.D. 125, a Greek named Aristides wrote to a friend about the new religion of those who had decided to look at life and death through the eyes of Christ: "If any righteous man among the Christians passes from this world, they rejoice and offer thanks to God, and they escort his body with songs and thanksgivings as if he were setting out from one place to another nearby." Five hundred years later, in A.D. 627, the court of King Edwin of Northumbria awaited the first Christian missionary to arrive in that area. His name was Paulinus. The old hall was blazing with torches. A crowd of eager listeners waited to hear what the visitor would say. A bearded old earl stood up in his place and asked, "Can this new religion tell us what happens after death? The life of man is like a swallow flying through this lighted hall. It enters in at one door from the darkness outside, and flitting through the light and warmth passes through the farther door into the dark unknown beyond. Can this new religion solve for us the mystery? What comes to men in the dark, dim unknown?" Maybe that old earl, like King David centuries before, was thinking of his boy killed in battle. King Edwin decided to look at death — and life — from the perspective of Jesus Christ. Edwin was baptized on Easter Eve, 627, at York in a wooden church which had been erected for the occasion.

The stages of grief are our "stations of the cross." Those stages have been mapped out by Dr. Elizabeth Kubler-Ross and others. Clearly, not only the dying, but those who are left here must go through the disbelief and denial, the anger and depression, and, we hope, the acceptance. Though we can meet grief by declaring it, by delighting with gratitude in happy memories, by dedicating ourselves to others who are hurting, and by deciding to look at death through the eyes of Christ, we cannot evade traveling through the dark valley of the shadow of death as those who grieve for souls whom we have loved and see no longer. The former Archbishop of Canterbury, Donald Coggan, has written about "the hard lesson of Christian prepositions — that the predominant preposition is not 'out of' but 'through' and 'in'. 'My strength is made perfect *in* weakness.' 'When thou passest *through* the waters, I will be with thee'." (Isaiah 43:2) The darkness of the valley of grief through which we must pass reminds us of the darkness on the hill of Golgotha. All griefs lead to the Cross. There, we find ourselves part of the company of those who mourn. We can entrust our departed to Christ.

Through all depths of pain and loss
Sinks the plummet of His Cross;
Never yet abyss was found
Deeper than that Cross could sound.

So, we leave them in His hands. Where better could we leave them?

2 Samuel 23:1-7

Proper 16
Pentecost 14
Ordinary Time 21

What Makes People Great?

David son of Jesse was the man whom God made great . . . (2 Samuel 23:1, TEV)

In a book titled *Irrepressible Churchill*, Kay Halle told the story of a little boy who lived near Chartwell, England. It was at Chartwell Manor that Winston Churchill lived after his retirement as prime minister in 1955. This little boy was taken to Chartwell by the woman who cared for him each day. She told the little boy that he was going to see "the greatest man in the whole, wide world." When this woman and the boy in her charge arrived at Chartwell Manor, they learned that Sir Winston had retired for his afternoon nap. While the woman was having tea, the little boy slipped away from the adults, climbed the stairs and started to explore the house. He pushed open the door to one of the bedrooms and saw Winston Churchill curled up in bed, ready for one of his famous naps. The little boy crept to the bed and asked, "Are you the greatest man in the whole wide world?" Sir Winston fixed his eye on him for a moment, then replied, "Of course, I'm the greatest man in the whole wide world. Now buzz off."

What makes people great? By the standards of our society, greatness appears to be based on four possible foundations: wealth, honors, fame, or power. The power may be physical, as in the agility and stamina of an athlete. The power may also be financial or political. In contrast to these sources of greatness, the author of the Second Book of Samuel traces greatness to God. In speaking about King David, the author wrote: "David son of Jesse was the man whom God made great, whom the God of Jacob chose to be king, and who was the composer of beautiful songs for Israel." (2 Samuel 23:1-2, TEV) The same God who inspired greatness in his servant David is the God who inspires greatness in you. "I am sure," wrote St. Paul, "that God who began the good work within you will keep right on helping you grow in his grace until his task within you is finally finished on that day when Jesus Christ returns." (Philippians 1:6, LB) There are four qualities to this divinely inspired greatness: humility, helpfulness, hopefulness, heroism.

I

First, a person is made great by being humble. When King David was a boy, he lived as a shepherd on the hills of Judea. Under the black sky, David saw the stars and realized how small human beings are. In a psalm ascribed to David are these words:

When I look at the sky, which
you have made,
at the moon and the stars
which you set in their
places —
what is man, that you think of
him;
mere man, that you care for
him?

Psalm 8:3-4, TEV.

It is only by recognizing our littleness that we ever discover anything big. Childhood is the time of physical littleness. To a child, everything is big. To a child, the world is filled with wonders. As G.K. Chesterton said: "The world will never starve for wonders; but only for want of wonders." The mental equivalent to the physical littleness of childhood is humility. That is why the Scriptures say: "Jesus called a child, had him stand in front of them, and said, 'I assure you that unless you change and become like children, you will never enter the Kingdom of heaven. The greatest in the Kingdom of heaven is the one who humbles himself and becomes like this child." (Matthew 18:2-4, TEV)

Sir Isaac Newton, the British scientist and mathematician, lived from 1642 to 1727. He gave the world three things: a new mathematics; a new insight into the nature of light; and a new understanding of the force which holds the universe together. Alexander Pope recognized his greatness when he wrote:

Nature and Nature's laws lay hid in Night:
God said, Let Newton be! And all was light.

Newton has been called "one of the greatest names in the history of human thought" because of his contributions to mathematics, physics and astronomy. Yet, listen to Newton, in the closing years of his life, as he described himself: "I do not know what I may appear to the world, but to myself I seemed to have been only like a boy playing on the seashore and diverting myself in now and then finding a smoother pebble or a prettier shell than ordinary, whilst the great ocean of truth lay all undiscovered before me." First of all, a person is made great when God inspires within him the virtue of humility.

II

Secondly, a person is made great by being helpful. When David was a boy, he was taken to the palace of King Saul. David's musical talents proved most helpful to the king. Scripture says: "Whenever the evil spirit came upon Saul, David would get his harp and play it. The evil spirit would leave and

Saul would feel better again and be all right." (1 Samuel 16:23, TEV) The music of David helped Saul to get over his black moods. Furthermore, the boy David was helpful to Saul in another way. While he was taking food to his brothers who were serving on the front lines in Israel's battle against the Philistines, David saw the Philistine giant, Goliath, and heard him taunt the army of Israel. David volunteered to fight the giant. King Saul offered David his royal armor, but after trying it on, David said, "I can't fight with all this. I'm not used to it." (1 Samuel 17:39, TEV) Instead, David used the most effective weapon he had. It was his shepherd's sling, a long, thin piece of cloth into which a stone was placed, swung around the head, and then one end released, hurling the stone at its target. Jewish shepherds were famous for their accuracy with a sling. "Everyone of them," says the author of the Book of Judges, "could sling a stone at a strand of hair and never miss." (Judges 20:16, TEV) By killing the Philistine giant, David proved most helpful to King Saul.

When Jesus spoke about greatness, he said, "If one of you wants to be great, he must be the servant of the rest." (Mark 10:43, TEV) Far from being an other-worldly platitude removed from our daily lives, our Lord's words underline a principle of all effective living: The person or the institution which serves most, is most helpful, is most useful, is the one that will survive and be counted great! Bruce Barton, the American advertising executive, reminded people that the basis on which the executives of an automobile agency will claim the financial support of its customers is that they will crawl under your car oftener and get themselves dirtier than any of their competitors. That company is willing to give more service. If it does, people will patronize it and it will be great. On the other hand, any company or institution which does not serve and prove useful to the public will fail.

III

Thirdly, a person is made great by being hopeful. When David became the king of God's people, he had great hopes which guided him like stars guide travelers in a strange land. For instance, David hoped to organize the twelve scattered tribes of Israel into a unity. That was his hope and he accomplished it. Again, he hoped to unite the north and the south into one strong political reality. That was his hope and he realized it by choosing a neutral city, midway between north and south. He captured this Jebusite city and today we know it as Jerusalem. Again, David hoped to capture the Ark from the Philistines, that Covenant Box in which the stone tablets bearing the Ten Commandments were kept. He succeeded in capturing that Ark and restoring it to Jerusalem. That Ark of the Covenant became the basis of the great Temple which David planned to build and which his son, Solomon, succeeded in building.

Great hopes make people great! That's why Alfred, Lord Tennyson spoke of "the mighty hopes that make us men." That's why Goethe said, "In all things it is better to hope than to despair." That's why old Samuel Johnson said, "It is worth a thousand pounds a year to have the habit of looking on the bright side of things." The children whom Christ called upon us to emulate know this. A man stopped to watch a Little League baseball game. He asked one of the youngsters what the score was. "We're behind eighteen to nothing," was the answer. "Well," said the man, "I must say you don't look discouraged." "Discouraged?" the boy said, puzzled. "Why should we be discouraged? We haven't come to bat yet."

IV

Fourthly, a person is made great by being heroic. When David stole Bathsheba from her husband, Uriah, then engineered his death, David entered one of the dark and damaging periods of his life. Maybe David felt that he was above the law, or that his particular affair with Bathsheba was somehow exempt from God's law. But, as Francis Thompson heard God say to a soul, "All things betray thee, who betrayest Me."

David's conscience and sense of social justice betrayed him. When Nathan the prophet appeared before the king and told a little story about a rich man who stole a poor man's only lamb, David became angry with the rich man and said, "I swear by the living Lord that the man who did this ought to die!" (2 Samuel 12:5, TEV) Nathan looked steadily at the king and replied, "You are that man." (2 Samuel 12:7, TEV) Although David had fallen far from his high calling and destiny, there was still something heroic about him. He did not try to evade Nathan's words. He did not offer excuses. "David said to Nathan, 'I have sinned against the Lord.' Nathan answered him, 'The Lord has laid on another the consequences of your sin; you shall not die, but . . .' " (2 Samuel 12:13, NEB) David was heroic, not only because he had the courage as a boy to fight a giant, but because he had the courage as a man to wrestle with himself, to admit that he had been wrong, and to make a fresh start in life.

David's heroism inspired heroism in his soldiers. They seem to fulfill the statement of Thomas Carlyle, "We cannot look, however imperfectly, upon a great man without gaining something from him." The Scriptures say, "These are the names of David's heroes." (2 Samuel 23:8, NEB) and then lists more than thirty heroic soldiers. Heroes affect us in four ways. First, a hero captures our attention. One of those heroes was a man named Benaiah "who went down into a pit and killed a lion on a snowy day." (2 Samuel 23:20, NEB) Because we face problems that stalk us like lions, we admire Benaiah, whose action captures our attention. Secondly, a hero crystallizes our intention. The lion that Benaiah faced strayed up from the area near the Jordan River and was stranded in a snowstorm. The presence of that lion was not under Benaiah's control. However, what Benaiah could control and what we can control is our reaction to the problems we face. That type of self-control is a personal goal worth developing. Benaiah's example helps us to crystallize just such an intention. Thirdly, a hero cultivates our retention. Although it was a snowy day and the lion was in a pit, Benaiah did not run away; he held his ground before the lion. Benaiah's courage in the face of unfavorable circumstances encourages our retention, our holding on when the going gets tough. As a Norwegian proverb says, "A hero is one who knows how to hold on one minute longer." Fourthly, a hero catalyzes our extension. Just as a certain substance can spark a chemical reaction, so a heroic figure causes us to enlarge our outlook and to expand our efforts toward our goals.

What makes people great? What makes you great? It is the fact that the same God who made David great can make you great. It is the fact that you are related to Jesus Christ, great David's greater Son. Through that continuing relationship which is at work in the center of your being, you are being given those qualities that make people great — the qualities of being humble, helpful, hopeful, and heroic. "My dear children, your life has its source in God, and yours is the victory . . . because the Spirit who is in you is greater than the spirit who is in the world." (1 John 4:4, Barclay)

1 Kings 2:1-4, 10-12

Proper 17
Pentecost 15
Ordinary Time 22

How Can We Foretell the Future?

"If you obey him, the Lord will keep the promise he made . . ." (1 Kings 2:4, TEV)

In 6,000 years, our descendants will open the Crypt of Civilization at Oglethorpe University in Atlanta, Georgia, and discover how twentieth century people lived. A president of the University, Dr. Thornwell Jacobs, created a vault in the Atlanta institution because he wanted people out there in the future, around the year 8,000, to have a "complete picture of how human beings lived and thought during the days of our generation." The date for the opening of the Crypt was chosen, because it represented a time in the future roughly equal to the length of recorded history to the year 1940 when the vault was welded shut. What will those people out there in the future find when they open the vault? Among other things, they will find a model of the Eiffel Tower, 800 books on microfilm, 11 tape-recorded hours of President Franklin Roosevelt's voice, seeds, a movie projector and a machine to teach English.

How fascinating it is to think about those people out there in the future rummaging through the souvenirs of the early twentieth century! How many other items we'd like to add to that collection to tell the story of the last generation! Most of us are interested in the future for more personal reasons than the remnants of our civilization. "My interest is in the future," said Charles F. Kettering of the General Motors Corporation, "because I'm going to spend the rest of my life there." That word *future* comes from the Latin word "futurus," the future participle of "esse" (to be). The word *future* signifies the time to come, the events that will happen.

Can we foretell the future? Traditionally in Christian theology, any attempt to learn the free future from a source other than God was considered the sin of divination. Since God alone knows what human beings will choose to do in the future, attempts to learn that future from a created source is a repetition of that sin which St. Paul mentioned when he wrote of those who "have offered reverence and worship to created things instead of to the Creator." (Romans 1:25, NEB) Nevertheless, human beings have always been so curious about the future that they have resorted to all sorts of methods to find out about that future. Among those methods are: consulting oracles, inspecting cards, studying the palm of the hand, examining the bumps on the head, watching the movement of the stars, plotting horoscopes, looking for messages from the spirits of the dead, using a ouija board.

Despite this divine prohibition against divination, people still want to know the future. When King David came to end of his life, he was concerned about the future. He looked back on his life and remembered the many parts he had played on the world's stage: the shepherd boy of the Judean hills; the great king of Israel; the thief who stole Bathsheba; the grieving father who mourned the death of his rebellious son, Absalom.

> *When David was about to die, he called his son Solomon and gave him his last instructions: "My time to die has come. Be confident and determined, and do what the Lord your God orders you to do. Obey all his laws and commands, as written in the Law of Moses, so that wherever you go you may prosper*

> *in everything you do.* If you obey him, the Lord will keep the promise he made . . ." *(1 Kings 2:1-4, TEV)*

Wasn't David talking about the future when he said to Solomon, "If you obey him [God], the Lord will keep the promise he made?" Notice that little word "if" in these words of the dying David to his son. That word "if" represents conditions to be met, requirements to be fulfilled, qualifications to be observed. We can, in part, foretell the future as we examine the conditions which affect the time to come. There are four conditions worth noting as we seek to foretell the future. Those conditions are: our concerns; our capabilities; our characteristic behavior; and our choices.

I

First, if we want to foresee a future bright with God's promise, we have to fulfill the condition of having the right concerns. Edmund Burke said, "Tell me what are the prevailing sentiments that occupy the minds of your young men, and I will tell you what is to be the character of the next generation." In April, 1986, Harold E. Wagoner, a leading architect of church buildings, died in his suburban Philadelphia home. Mr. Wagoner and his architectural firm, Wagoner and Associates, designed more than 600 churches across the United States. Among them were the Church Center at the United Nations in New York City, the interior of the Air Force Academy Chapel in Colorado Springs, the National Presbyterian Church in Washington, D.C., and the Westwood Methodist Church in Los Angeles. Speaking of his work, Harold Wagoner said, "The great thing about being an architect is that you can walk into your dreams." An architect is the person who designs and lays out plans of buildings, and then sees that these plans are followed by the workers who put up the buildings.

David's son, Solomon, was an architect. It was during his reign as king that he was the architect, the chief builder, of the Temple in Jerusalem. Solomon realized that each person is the architect of his own future. In a collection of proverbs ascribed to him are these words: "Be careful how you think; your life is shaped by your thoughts." (Proverbs 4:23, TEV) To a larger extent than we often realize, each of us walks into his dreams. Those dreams are the dominant concerns in our minds. As John Burroughs said: "If you have a thing in mind, it is not long before you have it in hand." How can we foretell the future? For one thing, we can check the dominant concerns in our minds, for they are the stuff out of which we build tomorrow:

Isn't it strange
That princes and kings,
And clowns that caper
In sawdust rings,
And common people
Like you and me
Are builders for eternity?

Each is given a bag of tools,
A shapeless mass,
A book of rules;
And each must make —
Ere life is flown —
A stumbling block
Or a stepping stone.

R. L. Sharpe

II

Secondly, if we want to foresee a future bright with God's promise, we have to fulfill the condition of developing our capabilities. A teacher told her class of sixth graders that John Milton, the poet, was blind. The next day she asked the children whether any of them could remember what Milton's great affliction was. "Yes," replied a little boy, "Milton's great affliction was that he was a poet." Writing poetry can be a painful affliction. T.S. Eliot called it "the intolerable wrestle with words and meanings." For an aspiring writer to develop the capability for poetry he finds in his personality, he must fulfill the conditions of study and intellectual discipline.

God has chosen to create his "poems" in a similar way. The word *poem* is derived from the Greek verb "poein." Originally, it meant to make something. In his Letter to Christians in Ephesus, Paul wrote: "For we are God's handiwork [in Greek, "poem"], created in Christ Jesus to devote ourselves to the good deeds for which God has designed us." (Ephesians 2:10, NEB) God has chosen to use human cooperation in the development of those talents, those capabilities, he has planted in our personalities. If, for example, we want to develop our capability to be physically healthy, we must cooperate with God. No doubt, theoretically, God could keep us strong without our having to eat, but he has chosen human cooperation as the means to grow food and to harvest that food for our use. Likewise, theoretically, God could keep us healthy without medicine and medical doctors, but he has chosen to preserve the poetry of healthy lives through human agents. As Augustine said: "Without God, we cannot; without us, God will not."

How can we foretell the future? We can check whether we are paying the price to develop the capabilities in our personalities we call talents. A teenage girl said to Marian Anderson, the world famous black contralto, "I'd give anything in the world if I could sing like that." The singer smiled and replied, "Would you give eight hours of practice a day?"

III

Thirdly, if we want to foresee a future bright with God's promise, we have to fulfill the condition of regulating our characteristic behavior. In his book *Talks To Teachers on Psychology*, William James has a chapter titled "The Laws of Habit." In it James wrote:

The drunken Rip Van Winkle, in Jefferson's play, excuses himself for every fresh dereliction by saying, "I won't count this time!" Well, he may not count it, and a kind of Heaven may not count it; but it is being counted none the less. Down among his nerve-cells and fibers, the molecules are counting it, registering and storing it up to be used against him when the next temptation comes. Nothing we ever do is, in strict scientific literalness, wiped out.

What William James wrote in 1899 is what St. Paul wrote over eighteen centuries earlier: "Do not deceive yourselves. No one makes a fool of God. A person will reap exactly what he plants." (Galatians 6:7, TEV)

How can we foretell the future? One way is to look at those characteristic forms of behavior that we call habits. This is what Frederick Hedge had in mind when he wrote: "Every man is his own ancestor, and every man is his own heir. He devises his own future, and he inherits his own past." The person who forms the habit of smoking in bed may one day make an ash out of himself. Nor is it too hard to foretell the future of the high-speed driver, the overeater, the overdrinker. We are clothed by our habits. That word *habit* is derived from the Latin word "habitus," meaning clothing. Our habits form the garments of our personalities. As John Dryden, the seventeenth century English writer, put it: "We first make our habits, and then our habits make us."

IV

Fourthly, if we want to foresee a future bright with God's promise, we have to fulfill the condition of making the right choices. Lowell Ditzen has recalled the days when Americans first started to travel by automobile. There were crude signs erected here and there to warn drivers of road conditions. One such sign, put up at the beginning of a long, mud road, frozen hard by the winter cold, read, "Watch the rut you start in. You'll be in it for the next thirty miles!" If we could borrow that sign and change the word "miles" to the word "years," what an insight it might give to some young person, trying to foretell his future: "Watch the rut you start in. You'll be in it for the next thirty years!'" Today's decisions are tomorrow's realities.

To choose is to make a decision. To decide means literally "to cut off." Imagine there are various alternatives hanging in front of you, like colored balls suspended by strings from the ceiling. The act of decision is the act of cutting one of those strings and letting that particular alternative be taken in hand. The words and example of Jesus underline the importance of making choices for our future. In the Parable of the Talents (Matthew 25:14-30), for example, the elements of risk and investment are shown to be as necessary in the religious dimension of life as they are in the business area. Or turn from his parables to the pattern of his life. Like Moses and Elijah before him, Jesus spent time at the beginning of his ministry weighing the alternatives that lay before him, counting the cost, and making the choices that would shape his future ministry. The importance of our choices in shaping our future can be seen in the fact that the word "choose" occurs 144 times in the Authorized Version of the Old Testament and twenty-four times in the New Testament. How can we foretell the future? Examine the direction of the choices in your will. "But, there are two sides to every question," objected one man who tried to minimize the importance of making choices. "Yes," said his friend, "and there are two sides to a sheet of flypaper, but it makes a big difference to the fly which side he chooses!"

God has two kinds of blessings. The one kind of blessing he gives us, whether we deserve it or not, "for he makes his sun to shine on bad and good people alike, and gives rain to those who do good and to those who do evil." (Matthew 5:45, TEV) The other blessing of God is conditional. It depends on whether we fulfill the conditions of that blessing. "If you obey him, the Lord will keep the promise he made," said David to Solomon. In this sense, we can foretell the future. The future which is filled with the blessings of God depends on our having the right concerns, on our developing our capabilities, on our regulating our characteristic behavior, and on our making the proper choices. As we face the future, then, remember how Christ used that little word "if" when he spoke of our happiness: "Now that you know this truth, how happy you will be *if* you put it into practice!" (John 13:17, TEV)

Proverbs 2:1-8

Proper 18
Pentecost 16
Ordinary Time 23

Where Can We Find Wisdom?

Look for [wisdom] as hard as you would for silver or some hidden treasure. (Proverbs 2:4, Today's English Version)

"Dad, have you cut all four of your wisdom teeth?" asked the teenager. "Yes, son," replied the father. "I have bought a used car, accepted a nomination, been chairman of the civic association, and married your mother." That man obviously thought that he had cut his "wisdom teeth" by chewing on four tough experiences. The four "third molars" have been given that name "wisdom teeth" because they usually appear during late adolescence or early adulthood. Wisdom, however, does not automatically come to us with the passing of the years or the accumulation of knowledge. As Bertrand Russell has said: "Wisdom is a harmony of knowledge, will, and feeling, and by no means necessarily grows with the growth of knowledge."

As far back as the days of Solomon in all his glory (and long before that!), wisdom was held in high esteem. God, however, gives people wisdom as he gives them precious metals; his treasure house is not the mint, but the mine. Because the quest for the best in effective living calls for an active, energetic search, the author of The Book of Proverbs wrote: "Look for [wisdom] as hard as you would for silver or some hidden treasure." (Proverbs 2:4, TEV)

The English word *wisdom* itself gives us a clue to the nature of this key for coping with the world. The word *wisdom* comes from the Old English word "wis," which meant wise. That word in turn came from the Latin word "videre," meaning to see. Our familiar term "video" comes from that same root. Wisdom, then, which means knowledge and good judgment based on experience, is a certain way of looking at life with the mind's eye. "Look for [wisdom] as hard as you would for silver or some other hidden treasure," advises Proverbs. As we ponder his words, we ask ourselves, "Where Can We Find Wisdom?" Let us explore the possibility that the prize which makes us wise is found in looking — looking behind, looking between, looking before, looking beyond.

I

First, we can find wisdom by looking behind. Sir Isaac Newton, the seventeenth century English scientist and mathematician, once hired a skilled mechanic to build a small mechanical replica of the solar system. A gold ball represented the sun; dull gray balls stood for the planets. By turning a crank, Sir Iaaac could make the model move, so that the tiny balls traced the orbits of the heavenly bodies. One day an atheistic friend of Sir Isaac came to see his work. The friend was fascinated by the mechanism which the great scientist was using for his investigation of the solar system. "This is marvelous!" exclaimed the visitor. "Who made it?" "No one," replied Sir Isaac. "It just happened. We had some balls, rods, and gears lying around and they got together and started going." Sir Isaac's friend found it hard to believe that the tiny model of the solar system arose by chance. Wisdom, then, looks behind the surface appearances of things to their causes. This is the wisdom which St. Paul had in mind when he wrote his Letter to the Christians in Rome: "Ever since God created the world, his invisible qualities, both his eternal power and his divine nature, have been clearly seen; they are perceived in the things that God has made." (Romans 1:20, TEV)."

When a person looks behind the surface appearances to the cause of an action, an event, or a thing, we call him "wise." For instance, at a construction site anyone could see laborers carrying wood and laying bricks. But, it is the wise architect who looks behind these actions to the idea which has inspired the work and measures its progress. Similarly, an ambulance driver would see the flushed face and feel the fevered body of a sick person he was called to transport. It is the wise physician who can look behind these symptoms to the cause of the illness.

We can look behind not only in a logical fashion; we can also look behind in a chronological way. We can find wisdom by reading and making our own the words of previous generations with their wealth of experience of God and the world. Nowhere is "the Communion of Saints" more evident than in the sharing of ideas between generations. Listen again to Sir Isaac Newton in a letter he wrote to Robert Hooke on February 5, 1675: "If I have seen further (than you and Descartes) it is by standing upon the shoulders of giants." With their help we can find wisdom by looking behind.

II

Secondly, we can find wisdom by looking between. In a certain grade school one week before Christmas, a cynical teacher hung a string across the top of the blackboard at the front of the classroom. The children thought that the teacher was going to put Christmas decorations on the string. The teacher, however, had different ideas. She placed large letters of the alphabet on the string, so that they spelled out the message, "GOD IS NOWHERE." One little girl in the classroom found wisdom by looking between the letters on the string and seeing another possibility. She had been well-taught the significance of the Christmas celebration. She had a different way of looking at things. While the teacher and the other children were out of the room for recess, she stood on the teacher's chair and made a slight change in the message by separating a few letters. When the other students took their seats again after recess, they had the happy surprise of an unexpected new message of good news on the string. Now the letters there spelled "GOD IS NOW HERE."

There has been an instructive dispute over the etymology of the word *religion*. Lactantius Firmianus, a Christian writer of the late third and early fourth centuries, traced the derivation of the word *religion* to the Latin word "religare," which means "to bind." "We are tied to God," wrote Lactantius, "and bound to him by the bonds of piety." A century later Aurelius Augustinus, better known as Augustine, the bishop of Hippo on the northern coast of Africa, traced the derivation to the Latin word "religere," to recover. "Having lost God through neglect," wrote Augustine, "we recover Him and are drawn to Him." Earlier than these Christian writers, however, is Marcus Tullius Cicero, the Roman orator and statesman, who lived in the century before Christ. Like the little girl who found wisdom by looking between the letters, Cicero took the word *religion* from "relegere," to reread. Cicero wrote: "Those who carefully took in hand all things pertaining to the gods are called *religiosi*, from *relegere*." Such persons look between the lines, as it were, and reread the meaning inherent in the events of life. Often, it is the tears of suffering which cleanse our eyes to see more clearly. As Aeschylus, the Greek dramatist, wrote: "He who learns must suffer. And even in our sleep pain that cannot forget falls drop by drop upon the heart, and in our own despair, against our will, comes wisdom to us by the awful grace of God." (*Prometheus Bound*, 1, 177)

III

Thirdly, we can find wisdom by looking before. Luther Burbank was an American plant breeder and horticulturist.

He developed many new trees and plants and improved existing ones. He found wisdom by looking before him and seeing in his mind's eye the possibilities in the common field daisy. These flowers were despised by farmers in the East. Looking before him and seeing far ahead, Burbank said, "I crossed it [the common field daisy] with a Japanese daisy and an English daisy and produced the Shasta daisy. The bloom of my Shasta daisy has grown as much as two feet in circumference and seven inches from tip to tip." Burbank had similar success with cactus. "I also took the despised Arizona Desert Cactus and bred out of it its poison and all of its spikes, and made it edible for horses and cattle." Why was Luther Burbank successful in looking before him and seeing the possibilities in flowers and plants? He testified to his own outlook in this way: "It is my theory that there are no outcasts in nature; everything has a use, and everything in nature is beautiful if we are eager to ennoble it. Every weed is a possible beautiful flower."

How similar was the wisdom of the Divine Gardener, our Lord Jesus Christ! When Mary Magdalene first saw the risen Christ in the garden of Joseph of Arimathea, she thought he was the gardener. Maybe that title is closer to the truth than we have realized. "Christ," wrote Paul, "is the wisdom of God." (1 Corinthians 1:24, TEV) In Christ we see the Divine Gardener who considered many a human weed and looked before him to the possible beautiful flower that person could become. In Lloyd C. Douglas' sermon, "The Mirror," Christ speaks to Zacchaeus, the despised tax collector of Jericho whom our Lord had befriended " 'Zacchaeus," said the carpenter gently, 'what did you see that made you desire this peace?' 'Good master [answered Zacchaeus] — I saw — mirrored in your eyes — the face of the Zacchaeus I was meant to be!' " John Oxenham has written about this dimensions of

God grant us wisdom in these coming days,
And eyes unsealed, that we clear visions see
Of that new world that he would have us build
To Life's ennoblement and his high ministry.

IV

Fourthly, we can find wisdom by looking beyond. In a certain classroom a professor took a piece of paper and taped it to the blackboard, so that the class could see it. With a felt-tip pen, he made a circle and colored it in with black. Turning to the class, he asked, "What do you see?" One student answered, "I see a black dot." Another student replied, "I see a circle colored black." A third student said, "I see a spot on the paper." With a smile the professor said, "Do you realize that no one has yet said that they see a piece of white paper!" Sometimes we are so hypnotized by some black spot, some negative element in our situation, that we fail to look beyond that spot to the positive elements which are also present.

Wisdom is found in looking beyond the present *circumstances*. The word circumstances means "that which stands around" us. Our present circumstances can surely be depressing. It is in such times that we need to remember the prophet Elisha. Elisha had warned the king of Israel about an ambush planned by the Syrians and their king. The Syrian king decided to capture the prophet. When he learned that Elisha was in Dotham, he sent a large force there with horses and chariots. They reached the town at night and surrounded it. "Early the next morning Elisha's servant got up, went out of the house, and saw the Syrian troops with their horses and chariots surrounding the town. He went back to Elisha and exclaimed, 'We are doomed, sir! What shall we do?' 'Don't be afraid,' Elisha answered. 'We have more on our side than they have on theirs.' Then he prayed, 'O Lord, open his eyes and let him see!' The Lord answered his prayer, and Elisha's servant looked up and saw the hillside covered with horses and chariots of fire all around Elisha." (2 Kings 6:15-17, TEV)

To see beyond the present circumstances to the invisible, powerful forces at work in our world is wisdom. For example, the forces of the atom were present when the caveman lived, but he did not see them. He did not see the possibilities that were at hand. The forces of electricity were present long before Ben Franklin flew his kite and had that electrifying experience. Although unseen, those electrical forces were present in our universe, awaiting discovery and use. Isn't it the same in our religious life? In one of the Eucharistic Prayers of *The Book of Common Prayer* used in the Episcopal Church is this petition addressed to God: "Open our eyes to see your hand at work in the world about us." (page 372) With God's help we can find the wisdom of looking beyond the present circumstances to those positive factors we are apt to overlook.

Christians believe that the wisdom we have been seeking has already sought us and been embodied in a unique human life. This is the wisdom which looks behind the things which have evolved to that Divine Intelligence which has been involved in the process from the beginning. This is the wisdom which looks between the lines of history and discerns a Divine Purpose running through the seemingly perplexing parade of events. This is the wisdom which looks before and sees the flowers of the future in the unpromising weeds of the present. This is the wisdom which looks beyond, "not on things which are seen, but on things that are unseen." (2 Corinthians 4:18, TEV) In one of his stories, "The Higher Pragmatism," the American writer O'Henry faced the question we are facing today: "Where Can We Find Wisdom?" Listen to his puns as he writes: "Where to go for wisdom has become a question of serious import. The ancients are discredited; Plato is boilerplate; Aristotle is tottering; Marcus Aurelius is reeling . . . Solomon is too solemn; you couldn't get anything out of Epictetus with a pick." O'Henry, it is appalling that you forgot Paul! Remember his words to the Christians in Corinth:

> *. . . Greeks look for wisdom; but we proclaim Christ — yes, Christ nailed to the cross; and though this is a stumbling-block to Jews, and folly to Greeks, yet to those who have heard his call, Jews and Greeks alike, he is the power of God and the wisdom of God (1 Corinthians 1:23, NEB)*

It is in Christ that we find the wisdom which looks back, looks between, looks before, and looks beyond.

Proverbs 22:1-2, 8-9

Proper 19
Pentecost 17
Ordinary Time 24

Will Names Never Hurt Us?

A good name is more to be desired than great riches; esteem is better than silver or gold. (Proverbs 22:1, NEB)

Mrs. Reginald VanGleason decided to give a cocktail party at her mansion for her friends. She called in Nora, her maid of many years, and said to her, "I want you to stand at the door of the drawing room. As my friends arrive, I want you to call the guests' names." Nora smiled broadly and replied, "Oh, thank you, ma'am, for twenty years I've been waiting to call your friends names." "To call a person names" means to abuse that person by calling him derogatory nicknames or insulting titles. A *name* to us is usually a convenient label that we put on persons, places, things, qualities, and actions for practical identification. In the period when the Bible was written, however, a name meant much more than merely a label. A person's name stood for the character, the essential nature of its bearer. According to *Strong's Exhaustive Concordance of the Bible*, the word "name" is used 1,085 times in tha Scriptures. The Bible often refers to the significance of a name. Esau complained about his brother, Jacob: "No wonder his name is Jacob." (The name sounds like the Hebrew word for "cheat".) Abigail said of her husband Nabal: "He is exactly what his name means — a fool." (1 Samuel 25:25) Whenever in the biblical record an important change happened in a person's life, often his name was changed: Abram became Abraham; Jacob became Israel; Simon became Peter; Saul became Paul. The phrase "the Name of God," then, stands for the nature, the character, the revealed personality of God.

"The average man," said Dale Carnegie, "is more interested in his own name than he is in all other names on earth put together." Because of this fact, Carnegie advised: "Remember that a man's name is to him the sweetest and most important sound in any language." In The Book of Proverbs are these words: "A good name is more to be desired than great riches; esteem is better than silver or gold." (Proverbs 22:1, NEB) With that sentence in mind, what are we to make of that childhood rhyme: "Sticks and stones will break my bones, but names will never hurt me"? Is that true? Will names never hurt us? Let us think about names. First, consider that bad names do hurt people. Secondly, consider that good names do help people.

I

First, bad names can be hurtful. Not long ago Esso, the Standard Oil Company of New Jersey, decided to find a name for their worldwide affiliates. They brought in a computer. They went through all the brand names in the world as they sought a new name which would begin with an E and have only two syllables. They did not want to duplicate any existing name. They collected 15,000 telephone directories. For three and a half years, the computer scanned the directories to eliminate possible names which already existed. Finally, the researchers came up with eight names which were not brand names from anywhere in the world. Among the eight that began with the letter E and were two syllables long were the names Exxon and Enco. The night before the selection was to be made the researchers were horrified to learn that Enco, one of the possible choices, was the Japanese word that meant "a stalled car." How would you like that for the name of your gasoline? With that information in mind, they chose the name Exxon. Enco would have been a bad name for this oil company's worldwide affiliates.

The damage that can be done by a bad name applies not only in the business world. It also applies in personal life. Glendon E. Harris has reported that children with unusual names are discriminated against in school. To support that conclusion, he cites the results of a test done in 1973 by Herbert Harari, a psychologist at the University of California at San Diego. Eighty elementary school teachers were handed eight essays to mark. The essays, done by fifth and sixth graders, were of identical quality. There was only one variable factor: the names of the students which appeared on the essays. Four of the essays were signed with common names Michael, David, Karen, and Lisa. The other four essays were signed with unconventional names — Elmer, Hubert, Bertha, and Adelle. When these essays of identical quality were marked by these teachers, those bearing the names "Michael" and "David" scored an average of a full letter grade higher than "Elmer" and "Hubert." Among the girls' names, "Karen" and "Lisa" received a point-and-a-half higher score than "Bertha."

A great many bad names, demeaning names, have been used in our generation to describe human beings. Desmond Morris wrote a book about human beings with the inglorious title, *The Naked Ape*. A marine biologist, Albert Szent-Gyorgi, wrote a book about man called *The Crazy Ape*. Albert Camus, in an influential essay, compared modern man to a character in Greek mythology named Sisyphus who was condemned by the gods to the meaningless, absurd task of rolling a stone up a hill only to have that stone repeatedly roll down again. These are the bad names which have been put on human beings in our generation. "A good name is more to be desired than great riches," wrote the author of the Book of Proverbs. "Esteem is better than silver or gold." But many of the major thinkers of our day have not given human beings a good name. The self-esteem of human beings has been lowered by the images of humanity prevalent in literature and drama.

FitzSimons Allison is a bishop of the Episcopal Church. In 1972 he wrote a book titled *Guilt, Anger, and God*. In that book Bishop Allison put his finger on "disesteem," a low sense of self-worth, as one of the major problems of our day. He described a fishing trip in which he once took part on the east coast. As he was ready to step into the boat, he said to the other men, "I'm afraid we're not going to catch anything today." One of the old fishermen rebuked him, "Don't put the bad mouth on this fishing trip." The bishop was intrigued by that expression. He learned that the term "bad-mouth" means to talk badly about someone or something, to criticize or run down by abusive language. In his book Bishop Allison cited Hiam Ginott, the author of *Between Parent and Child*, who wrote about the importance of how we talk to children. He showed how bad names can mortally wound a child's self-esteem. To bad-mouth a child, to put a bad name on the child, is so harmful that the bishop has coined a phrase for that type of behavior. He calls it "psychic homicide." You can kill a person's sense of self-esteem by bad names.

II

Secondly, good names are helpful. Some years ago the orange growers of southern California wanted a good name for their oranges. There was a word which was being used by people who grew raisins, prunes, and other dried fruit, as well as by some of the orange growers. These California orange growers saw the advantage of having exclusive use of this name for their product. They approached the growers of the other fruits and bargained for that name. When the deal was completed, the orange growers paid $1,250,000 for the name "Sunkist." When they turned over that large sum of money, it was obvious from their behavior that "a good name is more to be desired than great riches; esteem is better than silver or gold." No doubt, that good name "Sunkist" and the good will it has engendered repaid those California orange growers many times over, but back then it was an act of faith in the power of a good name!

The value of a good name can be seen in the life of General Robert E. Lee, the great general who commanded the Confederate Army during the Civil War. After the Civil War, a group of men approached Lee. The group wanted to use Lee's name for a business enterprise and offered him a large sum of money for the right to use it. Lee was silent for several moments, then answered, "If my name is so valuable, then I must be very careful how I use it." Lee refused to sell his name. Instead, he became the president of Washington College at Lexington, Virginia. This small college had been badly damaged by the war. Reflecting on his life, General Robert E. Lee said, "I have led the young men of the South in battle; I intend to give the remaining years of my life in training them to do their duty in the time of peace." Nearly 3,000 years ago the author of Proverbs wrote: "A good name is more to be desired than great riches; esteem is better than silver or gold."

Between 1605 and 1615 Miguel de Cervantes, the Spanish author, wrote a book about an aged idealist named Don Quixote and his comrade Sancho Panza. Don Quixote set out on a campaign to restore the age of chivalry, to battle evil, and to right all wrongs. When Don Quixote arrived at a roadside inn, he met a bar maid and prostitute named Aldonza. He never called her by that name. Instead, he "good-mouthed" her. He envisioned her and named her Dulcinea, his ideal of a lady. Aldonza was bewildered by the old man's behavior. After she has been raped by men at the inn, she shouted at Don Quixote in anger and disillusionment, "Oh, don't call me a lady. I'm only a kitchen slut reeking with sweat. A strumpet men use and forget . . . I'm only Aldonza. I am nothing at all!" Nevertheless, Don Quixote kept on treating her and naming her as a person of genuine value. By the end of the story, he had succeeded in transforming Aldonza into Dulcinea, the fine

person he reckoned her to be, by the power of a good name. "A good name is more to be desired than great riches; esteem is better than silver or gold."

The good name that Don Quixote put on Aldonza is the opposite of the act of "bad-mouthing" another person. He "good-mouthed" her, regarded her and treated her as good and upright. He named her a person of wholesomeness and integrity. Reflecting on the value of a good name, Bishop Allison wrote: "Every enterprise I know that frees people from hang-ups — from Alcoholics Anonymous to group therapy — is at bottom an attempt to good-word a person, enabling him to accept himself by being accepted." The New Testament word for this "good-mouthing" is *logidzomai*, meaning to regard and treat as good. That word appears in Paul's Letter to the Christians in Rome as the word *reckon*: "Reckon yourselves as dead unto sin." (Romans 6:11) To reckon ourselves in this way and to give ourselves a good name is to consider ourselves of a certain value. We become able to "good-mouth" ourselves in this way because God has reckoned us to be good and acceptable in company with Jesus Christ: ". . . to the praise of the glory of His grace, by which He has made us accepted in the Beloved." (Ephesians 1:6, NKJV)

The classic example of one who used the power of a good name is Christ. In the records we have about Christ, we see him using good names to build up the person's sense of worth. For example, among his twelve apostles was a weak, vacillating, undependable man named Simon. What did Jesus do for this man? He gave him a good name, a nickname. Christ renamed this shifting, sandlike, big fisherman by calling him "Rocky." That is the meaning of Simon's new name which we know as "Peter." Silver or gold Christ had not, but what he did have he gave to Simon. He gave him the undeserved gift of an unexpected lift through a new name. Isn't this what Isaiah of Babylon meant when he wrote, "You will be called by a new name, a name given by the Lord himself"? (Isaiah 62:2, TEV) What a lift that must have been for Simon because "a good name is more to be desired than great riches; esteem is better than silver or gold!"

Christ did the same thing over and over again for people whom he met. Recall, for example, the woman who was caught in the act of adultery and dragged before Christ by Scribes and Pharisees who wanted to use this abused woman as a trap to ensnare our Lord. When Christ saw the bystanders weighing the stones in their hands, the stones with which to kill this lawbreaker, he said to them, "He who is without sin among you, let him throw a stone at her first." (John 8:7, NKJV) The crowd of accusers dissolved as one by one, beginning with the oldest, the men dropped their stones and left the scene. Then, for the first time in the encounter, Christ addressed her. Think of the names he could have used. Instead of using the bad, hurtful names people have created, he chose to dignify her by the power of a good name: " 'Woman, where are those accusers of yours? Has no one condemned you?' She said, 'No one, Lord.' And Jesus said to her, 'Neither do I condemn you; go and sin no more.' " (John 8:10-11, NKJV) Again, remember how Jesus traveled through the city of Jericho. In that place was a man named Zacchaeus, who was the superintendent of taxes. Such Jewish tax collectors, willing helpers of the hated Roman occupation force, were despised by their fellow Jews who would not accept their testimony in court nor their money in the synagogues. When Christ spotted Zacchaeus, who had gone out on a limb to see this popular figure, our Lord invited himself to dinner at the tax collector's home. When the townspeople saw Christ befriend this man, they put Zacchaeus down by placing on him the bad name of "sinner." But Christ, on the other hand, lifted this despised man up by the gracious gift of a good name. Christ said of him: ". . . for this man too is *a son of Abraham*." (Luke 19:9, NEB) How well Christ knew "a good name is more to be desired than great riches; esteem is better than silver or gold." Great riches Zacchaeus had, but how much more valuable to him was the good name he received from Christ.

"Man lives by affirmation even more than by bread," said Victor Hugo. Yet, how important is the basis of that affirmation! The *National Geographic* magazine once reported that an old man named Candelario found a $700 gold nugget in the gulches of Sandia Peak, near Albuquerque. "As soon as my luck was known," he said, "I became Don Candelario; within a week I was Don Juan Candelario; then Don Juan de Candelario, Caballero. My name grew for three weeks, till my gold was gone. Then I became simply Old Candelario again." That old fellow enjoyed a good name for almost a month, but it didn't last. How human it was for him to want that good name! "A good name is more to be desired than great riches; esteem is better than silver and gold." (Proverbs 22:1, NEB) Yet, how undependable was the basis of that old fellow's good name. The affirmation he received from other people was based on his monetary worth. In contrast to that, it is the glory of the Gospel that in a world where many factors today conspire to put us down, Christ lifts us up by putting on us a good name and raising our sense of self-esteem: "You are salt . . . light for all the world." (Matthew 5:13, 14, NEB) And best of all for our good name is this: "You are my friends." (John 15:15, NEB)

Job 28:20-28

Proper 20
Pentecost 18
Ordinary Time 25

How Can We Live Wisely?

"And he declares to man, 'For you to revere me is your wisdom, to shun evil that is knowledge." (Job 28:28, Moffatt)

When you think of Christ, do you see him as an idealist or as a realist? There are those who see him as primarily an idealist because he talked about love in an unlovely world. He talked about forgiveness in an unforgiving world. He talked about goodness in an evil world. He talked about a loving heavenly Father in a world of earthquakes, fire, flood, and other natural disasters. How then do you see Christ? Was he an idealist or was he a realist? I believe there is a neglected side to Christ's personality. While it is true that he talked about love, forgiveness, and peace, he also talked about wisdom. Sometimes he said to his listeners who heard but did not put his words into practice, "You are acting foolishly." Some people feel there is something exciting, adventurous, romantic, and light-hearted about being called a "sinner" instead of being called a saint. However, it is a different story, isn't it, when someone calls you foolish? Listen to how Jesus summed up The Sermon on the Mount:

"So then, anyone who hears these words of mine and obeys them is like a wise man who built his house on rock. The rain poured down, the rivers flooded over, and the wind blew

> *hard against that house. But it did not fall, because it was built on rock.*
>
> *"But anyone who hears these words of mine and does not obey them is like a foolish man who built his house on sand. The rain poured down, the rivers flooded over, the wind blew hard against that house, and it fell. And what a terrible fall that was!" (Matthew 7:24-27, TEV)*

How then can we live wisely? For an answer to that question, we turn to one of the great books in the Wisdom literature of Israel. In a significant passage in the Book of Job, Wisdom is seen as being God's possession. That Wisdom lies behind the created world, as the meaning behind it, the purpose running through it, and the goal to which it moves. Because we are within the created universe, we cannot see the whole meaning of God's purpose. It is here that the Book of Job says: "And [God] declares to man, 'For you to revere me is your wisdom, to shun evil — that is knowledge.' " (Job 28:28, TEV) If we take these words as our starting point, then we can answer the question about living wisely with four key words. To live wisely is to revere, to review, to revise, and to reverse.

I

How can we live wisely? First, to live wisely is to revere. The word *revere* comes from two Latin words that mean "to stand back in awe of something, or someone." It is to have a sense of wonder. For example, think of Moses. About 1,300 years before Christ Moses escaped from Egypt. He had murdered an Egyptian foreman who was mistreating a Hebrew slave. In his self-imposed exile, Moses became the shepherd of Midian, caring for the flocks of Jethro, his father-in-law. One day as he was caring for his flock, he saw in the distance a bush on fire. In the fall of the year in eastern Pennsylvania where I live, many a tree looks as though it were on fire because its leaves are orange and red and yellow. Such a sight makes one pause to contemplate it. Moses went to the bush and in his consciousness he heard God addressing him: "Take off your sandals, because you are standing on holy ground. I am the God of your ancestors, the God of Abraham, Isaac, and Jacob." (Exodus 3:5-6, TEV) Moses was instructed to live wisely by revering God in his creation. He had a sense of wonder and awe at the mysteries of life. As Elizabeth Barrett Browning wrote:

Earth's crammed with heaven
And every common bush afire with God;
But only he who sees takes off his shoes,
The rest sit round and pluck blackberries.

G. K. Chesterton once said, "The world will never starve for wonders, but only for want of wonder." Thomas Carlyle wrote: "The man who cannot wonder is but a pair of spectacles behind which there are no eyes." William L. Stidger recalled the day when a student found Pierre Curie, the French scientist, bending low over his microscope. The student thought that he had discovered his professor at prayer. He was ready to leave the room quietly when the scientist raised his head and turned. "Excuse me, sir," said the student, "I though you were praying." Pierre Curie again leaned over to peer through his microscope. As he did so, he said, "All science, research, and study is a prayer; a prayer that God will reveal his eternal secrets to us. For God does have secrets which he reveals only when man searches reverently for them . . . Research is always a prayer if it is done reverently." In the Baptism Service of the Episcopal Church, water is poured on the child's head and the sign of the cross is drawn on the child's forehead. Then, in the prayer which follows immediately after the actual act of baptizing, we ask God for several gifts for the child. The last of these gifts is requested in these words: "Give him . . . the gift of joy and wonder in all your works." (The Book of Common Prayer, page 308) To live wisely is, first, to live with a sense of reverence and wonder.

II

Secondly, to live wisely is to review our choices. If you were to go to a courtroom in the city of Venice, Italy, you would find a peculiar custom observed in the trial of a person accused of a capital crime. When a person is found guilty of a capital crime, there is a moment of silence in the courtroom. A figure enters the court dressed in a long black cloak. He walks solemnly to the center of the courtroom, faces the judges, and says these words: "Remember the baker!" That custom has grown out of an incident which happened three hundred years ago in that city. In those days, a baker was condemned to death for a crime. He was executed, but later his judges discovered that the baker was innocent of the crime for which he was put to death. The judges gave a sum of money to the city of Venice as an endowment fund. The interest from that money was to be used for two purposes. First, a perpetual light was hung in the palace of the Doges. That light was called "The Lamp of Expiation." Secondly, a man was to be hired to appear in the courtroom whenever a person was convicted of a capital crime. His appearance before the judges was to remind them of the wrong done by judges like themselves who had found an innocent man guilty. "Remember the baker!" said this mysterious black robed figure. His words called upon the judges to review their decision regarding the prisoner before them.

It is important for us to review our choices, if we are to live wisely. C. S. Lewis once wrote these words on the importance of our choices: "Every time you make a choice you are turning the central part of you, the part that chooses, into something a little different from what it was before. And taking your life as a whole, with all your innumerable choices, you are slowly turning this central thing either into a heavenly creature or into a hellish creature . . ."

A major league baseball umpire remarked that he could never understand how crowds in the grandstands, hundreds of feet away from the plate, could see better and judge more accurately than he could, when he was only seven feet away from homeplate. Then, he added these words, "Sometimes, in life, we call 'strikes' on a person when we're really too far away to understand. Maybe, if we had a closer view of that person and his problems, we would review our choice to call him "out." We would give him the "benefit of the doubt," that is, we would make a favorable judgment about him when the proof of that person's blame or guilt is inconclusive. To live wisely is to have the humility to review our choices.

III

Thirdly, to live wisely is to revise our plans from time to time. Some years ago *True* magazine gave author Max Gunther an unusual assignment. Gunther was to find two men born about the same year with similar family backgrounds and economic conditions. Then he was to research and write an article to show how these two men lived in such a way that one remained in poverty and obscurity, while the other went on to wealth and fame. Max Gunther began his research in New York City's Bowery district, the "skid row" of men who were drunken, jobless, and hopeless. In the Majestic Bar, he talked with many men. After those interviews, he went to the New York Public Library where he read many volumes of *Who's Who in America* until he found a man whose background matched one of those men on "skid row."

Both men were born in Amsterdam, New York, during World War I. They grew up in the lower-class east end of that city. Both men were highly intelligent. Their fathers were immigrant laborers. Both families were poor economically and with no social standing. The first man was Charles Alexander Wilson. He enlisted in the army on June 15, 1950. Ten days after he entered the service, the Korean War started and he was sent to Korea. Looking back on that time in his life, Wilson reflected, "I figured nothing I do is ever going to turn out right. I figured from now on the hell with it. Korea is where I started drinking in earnest." When he returned to New York in the late 1950s, he squandered his discharge pay. Someone told him where to get a free meal and bed tickets in Bowery hotels. That choice to go to the Bowery changed Wilson's life. "When I got my free meal that night and went to bed in a free dormitory," he told author Max Gunther, "I just gave up. The pressure was off. I didn't have to hunt for a job anymore. From that day on, I was trapped." Think how different his story would have been if he had reviewed his choices and revised his actions!

The second man chosen by Max Gunther for his article was Issur Danielovitch. He could have followed his father as a laborer, but he revised his plans, and decided to go to college. He had to work in a department store in Amsterdam to pay his tuition and expenses through school. He joined the Navy in 1942. When he returned to civilian life, he revised his plans again and headed for Hollywood where he appeared in small, unimportant parts in several motion pictures. He finally was offered a lucrative role in an expensive production by a major motion picture studio. He thought he would accept that offer, but then he revised his plans and appeared in a low-budget, low-salary film called "Champion." Issur Danielovitch wisely reviewed and revised his life choices several times. That is why the world knows him today as the successful and respected actor, Kirk Douglas.

IV

Fourthly, to live wisely is to reverse direction from time to time. There was a teacher of first grade children who had forty children in her class. One rainy day all those forty children wore boots to school to protect their feet from the rain.

That morning the teacher struggled to remove forty pairs of boots for the children. At noontime she pushed forty pairs of feet into those same boots, so the children could go home for lunch and again struggled to remove them when they came back to school for the afternoon class. At the end of the day, she sighed with relief as she Pushed the last pair of boots on little Freddie Jones. As she gave the final tug to Freddie's boots, he said to her, "These boots aren't mine." The teacher groaned and pulled the boots off Freddie's feet and put them on the floor. Freddie watched all this in silence, then said to the teacher, "They're not mine. They're my sister's, but my mother said I had to wear them today!"

That poor teacher had to reverse the direction of her activity again. In far more important matters, to live wisely is often to reverse the whole direction in which our lives have been moving. This need to reverse direction takes us right up into the heart of Christ's teachings. In William Barclay's splendid translation of the New Testament is this incident reported in Matthew's version of the story of the Good News: "Jesus called a little child, and made him stand where they could all see him. 'I tell you truly,' he said, 'unless you change the whole direction of your lives, and become like little children, you will certainly not get into the Kingdom of Heaven at all.' " (Matthew 18:2-3, Barclay)

Recall those words from The Book of Job: "And [God] declares to man, 'For you to revere me is your wisdom, to shun evil — that is knowledge.' " (Job 28:28, Moffatt) This shunning of evil, this reversing of direction by turning away from self-destructive paths, is the appeal behind those familiar scriptural invitations to "repent," to be "converted," "to be transformed by the renewing of your mind." To live wisely is to sometimes put our lives into reverse. "It is never too late," said George Eliot, "to be what you might have been." It is never too late to turn in reverence to God and to turn away from evil.

Every day is a new beginning,
Listen, my soul, to the glad refrain.
And despite past sins, and puzzles forecasted,
and possible pain,
Take heart, you can begin again!

"If any of you falls short in wisdom," wrote James, "he should ask God for it and it will be given him, for God is a generous giver who neither refuses nor reproaches anyone." (James 1:5, NEB) What is it which God will give so that we can live wisely? He will give us the wisdom to revere the mystery and wonder of life. He will give us the wisdom to review our choices. He will give us the wisdom to revise our plans from time to time. He will give us the wisdom to reverse our direction when we've been on the wrong track. "And he declares to man, 'For you to revere me is your wisdom, to shun evil that is knowledge.' " (Job 28:28, Moffatt)

Job 42:1-6

Proper 21
Pentecost 19
Ordinary Time 26

Is Your Religion Second-Hand?

"In the past I knew only what others had told me, but now I have seen you [God] with my own eyes." (Job 42:5, TEV)

"Second-hand Sam" was horrified to see a recent customer drive back into his used car lot. Just an hour before, that customer had bought one of Sam's "second-hand specials." Sam stood in the doorway of his trailer and called across the lot, "Nothing wrong, is there?" The man who had bought the car shouted back, "No, I just wanted to return some things. Remember that you said this second-hand car was only driven to the bank once a week by a little old lady? Well, that little old lady left some cigars in the glove compartment and a bottle of Scotch under the front seat!"

Sam called his cars "second-hand" because another hand had first driven them. That word "second-hand" means not new, used or worn already by someone else. The word often has shady associations. For instance, in 1921, Grant Clarke wrote a song titled "Second-Hand Rose":

Chorus

I'm wearing second-hand hats, second-hand clothes,
That's why they call me Second-Hand Rose.
Ev'ryone knows that I'm just Second-Hand Rose
From Second Avenue.

Like a used car and the possessions of Second-Hand Rose, one's religious faith can be second-hand, too. In one sense, all of us began our religious life with a second-hand faith. As Dr. Harry Emerson Fosdick wrote in *A Faith for Tough Times*:

> *We hear about Christian faith and life before we experience it; in family and church we accept its expressions before we vitally see for ourselves its meaning. As we hear, and in a way believe, that Beethoven is a great musician before we are inwardly, intimately captivated by him, so in every important realm second-hand acceptance precedes first-hand experience.*

The very word "tradition" means literally something handed down. In his Letter to the Christians in the Greek city of Corinth, St. Paul wrote: "First and foremost, I handed on to you the facts which had been imparted to me." (1 Corinthians 15:3, NEB) Paul used a traditional Jewish expression to stress the fact that he was passing on a tradition which existed before his own ministry. However, it is crucial to a vital faith that our traditional acceptance become a lively apprehension. It is by such a development that we grow from a second-hand inheritance to a first-hand experience. "What you have inherited from your fathers," said Goethe, "you must earn for yourself before you can call it yours."

What is it that makes that transformation possible? I suggest three verbs to summarize the factors which change religious faith from a second-hand inheritance to a first-hand experience. Those words are: wrestle, welcome, and wonder.

I

First, consider the word "Wrestle." Our religious faith is changed from a second-hand inheritance to a first-hand experience when we wrestle with religious questions. That is what one Bible character named Job did. His religion had been inherited. It was of the second-hand variety. In times of prosperity, the traditional theology of his day was satisfactory. But, when Job suffered the strokes of destitution, pain, rejection by society, and his own sense of separation from God, the old neat religious formulas were not enough. Job had to wrestle with two issues: first, there was his conviction that God was just in his dealings with human beings; secondly, there was his conviction that the personal sufferings he was undergoing represented an injustice.

The Book of Job was written by an author who was challenging the orthodox religious teaching of that day. Like Rabbi Harold S. Kushner of our own day, that ancient author also felt troubled "when bad things happen to good people." The accepted teaching in those days was based on a simple equation: if you had misfortune in your life, if you suffered an accident or had bad health, it was directly due to personal sin on your part. The author of the Book of Job believed that this neat formula oversimplified the facts of life. Sometimes, of course, it is true that personal sin does cause personal suffering. For instance, when a person abuses the laws of health, he usually suffers from that abuse. However, argued this author, to trace all personal suffering to personal sin is an oversimplification. In this dramatic story from the Old Testament, Job wrestled with the loss of his children, his property, and his health. Job steadfastly refused to admit that he had done anything to justify such dreadful suffering as he endured. After several rounds of sparring with his three "comforters," Eliphaz, Bildad, and Zophar, the Book reached its climax when God overwhelmed Job with the mysteries of creation:

Has the rain a father?
Who sired the drops of dew?
Whose womb gave birth to the ice,
and who was the mother of the frost
from heaven . . .?
Can you bind the cluster of the
Pleiades
or loose Orion's belt?
Can you bring out the signs of the
zodiac in their season . . . ?

Job 38:28-32a, NEB

Until that dazzling encounter with the Divine, Job's knowledge of God had been a theoretical one he had received by the reports of others. But, after his vivid personal experience of God's overwhelming presence, he recognized the limitations of his understanding. Furthermore, he admitted that God's governing of the universe went beyond systems of justice known to men. "In the past I knew only what others had told me," Job said to God, "but now I have seen you with my own eyes. So I am ashamed of all that I have said, and repent in dust and ashes." (Job 42:5-6, TEV)

Your religious faith will be transformed from a second-hand inheritance to a first-hand experience as you wrestle with the religious questions imbedded in the hurts and problems you now face.

II

Secondly, consider the word "Welcome." Our religious faith is changed from a second-hand inheritance to a first-hand experience when we welcome new religious insights. Midway in the Holy Land of Christ's day, between Galilee in the north and Judea in the south, lay the nation of Samaria. There was an age-old quarrel between the Samaritans and the Jews. As John reminded his readers, "Jews will have nothing to do with Samaritans." (John 4:9, TEV) At one point in Christ's life he wanted to enter a Samaritan village. However, that village refused him entrance. (Luke 9:53) Two of Christ's friends, James and John, became so angry with the Samaritans' inhospitality that they wanted to call fire down from heaven to destroy that place. Maybe that is why Christ nicknamed those two men "the Sons of Thunder." (Mark 3:17) This Samaritan village did not welcome Christ. Because of that refusal, their knowledge of Christ remained a second-hand thing.

There were other Samaritans, however, who did welcome Christ. They had heard about him from an infamous woman of their village. That woman had gone to the well in Sychar at noon to draw water. For her to go to the well in the heat of the day was unusual for an Eastern woman. Christ made such an impression on this woman that she hurried back to the village and said to the people, "Come and see a man who has told me everything I ever did. Could this be the Messiah?" (John 4:29) Those people of the village Sychar welcomed new religious insights. Because of their hospitality of mind, they passed from a second-hand grasp of Christ to a first-hand experience. Hear the pride in their voices as they say to the woman of the well: "We believe now, not because of what you said, but because we ourselves have heard him, and we know that he really is the Savior of the world." (John 4:42, TEV)

Welcoming new religious insights transforms religious faith from a second-hand inheritance to a first-hand experience. That shouldn't surprise us, should it? Our lives are decisively shaped by our hospitality — or lack of it — to new ideas! In 1868 this item appeared in a New York newspaper:

> *A man has been arrested in New York for attempting to extort funds from ignorant and superstitious people by exhibiting a device which he says will convey the human voice any distance over metallic wires, so that it can be heard by the listener at the other end. He calls this instrument a telephone. Well-informed people know that it is impossible to transmit the human voice over wires."*

About that time, Mark Twain made a vow that he would never again invest in the new, strange inventions that kept coming his way. Shortly after he made that decision, Mark Twain was approached by a young man who asked him to buy stock in his new invention. When Twain refused, the young man left, disappointed. His name was Alexander Graham Bell and he had just invented the telephone!

III

Thirdly, consider the word "Wonder." Our religious faith

is changed from a second-hand inheritance to a first-hand experience when we wonder at the religious dimensions of human life. In Christ's day, there were those who saw in him a dimension of divinely royal kingship. Those persons who were privileged to have that insight wondered at this religious dimension in the otherwise thoroughly human life of the Man from Nazareth. Over the centuries, there have been those who have had that same experience. Whenever persons have wondered in this way, their faith has gone from being a second-hand inheritance to being a first-hand experience.

Recall that Friday morning in the spring of the year A.D. 30 when Pontius Pilate, the Roman governor, confronted Christ. After listening to the charges made against Christ by his enemies, Pilate went into his headquarters again. He summoned Christ and asked, "Are you the King of the Jews?" Some of Christ's contemporaries interpreted that religious dimension of Christ in political terms. Such an interpretation worried Pilate. Listen to Christ's answer: "Are you saying this because you have discovered it yourself, or because other people told you that I am?" (John 18:34, Barclay) Pilate, is this a second-hand opinion which you have inherited or is it a first-hand faith you have discovered as you yourself have wondered at the religious dimension of my life? That is what Christ's question implies. Over a year before that day when Christ faced Pilate, he put the same question to his disciples. First, Christ asked them about the second-hand opinions of the public: "Who are people saying that I am?" (Mark 8:27, Barclay) After listening to their answers, Christ put the question to them directly: " 'And you,' he asked them, 'who do you say I am?' " (Mark 8:29, Barclay) By that question, we are challenged to wonder, to think about, to explore the religious dimension in the human life of Jesus Christ. That act of wondering transforms our faith from a second-hand inheritance to a first-hand experience. Like Job, we end our exploration of Christ by saying, "In the past I knew only what others told me, but now I have seen you with my own eyes." (Job 42:5, TEV)

Paul Hovey recounted a discussion about the Bible. A woman in the group said, ''I let the preacher read the Bible for me. He understands it so much better than I do.'' Another person in the group commented, ''That's like buying second-hand clothes or being content with leftover food at a restaurant. Anyone who relies on the preacher to do his Bible reading for him will never have anything but a second-hand religion.'' Your religious faith will be transformed from a second-hand inheritance to a first-hand experience as you wrestle with religious questions, welcome religious insights, and wonder at the religious dimension of daily life.